www.islington.gov.uk

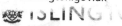

ISLINGTON

T 020 7527 6900

Library & Cultural Services

This item should be returned on or before the las...
Users who do not return items promptly may be l...
When renewing items please quote the number o...

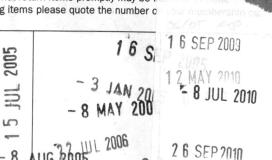

Contents

27 27 7 Siena

Listings

About the author

Rebecca Ford worked in public relations and advertising for several years before becoming a full-time travel writer and photographer. Her travels now take her all over the world. Her work has appeared in newspapers such as the *Independent*, the *Guardian*, the *Daily Express* and *Scotland on Sunday*. She writes and contributes to many other guidebooks, and also writes about walking, wildlife and railway journeys.

Acknowledgements

Rebecca would like to thank the following people: Lorenza and all the staff at the Hotel Santa Caterina in Siena; Gioia Milani and Federica Rossi, Pamela Monteverdi and Stefano Meacci, Giorgia Scarpelli, Chiara Baldanzi and Annie Adair, Ilaria Simonelli-Santi, Roberto Rappuoli, Valentina Pierguidi, all at Casa Pippo, Andrea Laurenzi and Paolo Ignesti. Thanks also to Paul Dwyer, the Siena APT, the Italian Tourist Board in London, and all the Italians who were so generous with their time and offers of reviving plates of pasta and cups of coffee.

It only takes a moment to be seduced by Siena but once you've succumbed you're under its spell for good. It's a Gothic gem and has everything you want from a medieval city: stern palaces, intimate alleyways and timeless churches, all grouped around a theatrically beautiful piazza – the Campo. Brushed in a soft reddish-brown – the burnt sienna of a painter's palette – even the city's bricks have character, burning deep red against a blue summer sky, mellowing to earthy hues as darkness falls. Traditions are alive here, a vigorous and vital part of daily life. Ancient buildings stand testament to medieval power struggles, the lofty tower of the civic Palazzo Pubblico rising cockily above the colossal, jazzily striped Cathedral. Within the churches and museums, blazing gold paintings speak of the days when Siena spawned a distinctive and dazzling school of art. And down the steeply sloping lanes and darkened, eerie alleyways lurks a compelling hidden city, quiet and full of secrets just waiting to be revealed to those who take the time to look.

Raw Siena

Appropriately, given its medieval architecture, Siena is most famous for staging a medieval spectacle – *Il Palio* – the bareback horse race that takes place each year in the Campo. It takes its name from the ancient prize, the *pallium*, a piece of precious cloth. Under searing temperatures, crowds jostle for position to watch this ritual, a pageant of costumed flag waving and drum beating that manifests not just ancient rivalries between the city's *contrade*, or districts, but also Siena's individuality, the distinct identity that sets it apart from the rest of Tuscany. Coming second doesn't count, it's only winning that matters and jockeys slash at one another, and their horses, in a vicious gallop for the finish. Tourists might flock to see it, but this event is not there for the benefit of visitors; it is run for the Sienese alone. Indeed many rather resent the attention from the outside world.

The heart of Tuscany

Siena's museums are stuffed with priceless works of art, but climb to the top of the Torre del Mangia and in the distance you'll see another of the city's treasures, its surrounding countryside. Just a short journey in any direction and you'll be in the sort of landscape that would inspire the most prosaic to poetry. Each village in this, the heart of Tuscany, has its own charms. To the north is Chianti, the hilly wine-growing region with its sleepy hamlets and dense woodlands of oak, juniper, chestnut and fragrant pine. To the east are picturesque towns filled with treats for art lovers, like Arezzo, Sansepolcro and Cortona. Travel west and you'll find the beguiling town of San Gimignano, a medieval dream of soaring towers that attracts a multitude of visitors each year. And south of Siena is the Tuscany of postcards, a rolling landscape of vineyards, cypress trees and sunflowers – and a scattering of pretty hilltop towns. Siena's countryside is as seductive as the city itself.

At a glance

Siena is the most compact of cities. It's built on three ridges that radiate out from the Piazza del Campo, rather like some mysterious, three-legged sea creature long embedded in a rock. Each leg forms one of the *terzi*, or thirds, into which the city has traditionally been divided. Everything is then neatly enclosed within a ring of well-preserved medieval walls.

Piazza del Campo

Il Campo is both the physical and emotional heart of the city. A shell-shaped, red-bricked piazza enclosed by a ring of glowering Gothic palaces, it's the most dramatic of spaces: an open-air theatre with just a hint of restrained medieval menace. It's the reference point for any visitor, and the backdrop to the city's best known event – the Palio. The focal point is the Palazzo Pubblico, an enormous edifice that acts as a monument to the glory days when Siena was a city state. With its imposing tower, the Torre del Mangia, it exerts a pull on both visitors and locals. People sit and chat and watch as the single hand moves slowly round the tower clock, the bricks change colour as the sun goes down – and time stands still. Around the Campo are bustling cafés and restaurants, their chairs and tables spilling onto the piazza's edge. In summer, when the red bricks in the centre are warmed by the heat of the sun, the Campo makes a convenient picnic spot and sometimes there's barely an inch of spare ground left on which to walk. Streets lead from here into the heart of each *terzo* and the different *contrade* – where the secret life of the city goes on in much the same way as it has for centuries.

Terzo di San Martino

Southeast of the Campo, this area is characterized by its Renaissance buildings; in particular the imposing Logge del Papa, its three great travertine arches quickly demanding attention.

★ **Ten of the best**

 Best

1   Palazzo Pubblico The imposing town hall on the Campo containing the civic museum; its famed frescoes are not to be missed, p32.

2   Palazzo Piccolomini and Museo delle Tavolette di Biccherna Siena's most underrated attraction: wooden ledgers exquisitely painted by some of the city's greatest artists, p37.

3   The Duomo An elaborate façade and jaw-dropping interior, colourful and crammed with treasures. Don't miss the Piccolomini Chapel or the Crypt (separate entrance), p42.

4   Museo dell'Opera del Duomo Pride of place goes to Duccio's *Maestà*, the work that essentially founded the Sienese school of painting, p45.

5   Spedale di Santa Maria della Scala The unalluring exterior conceals fascinating secular frescoes in the former hospital ward, p49.

6   Val d'Orcia and the Crete Senesi Picturesque hill towns, fields of sunflowers and sensuous cypress trees south of Siena. Everything you want from Tuscany, p63.

7   Abbazia di Monte Oliveto Maggiore Gloriously isolated abbey with cloisters smothered in frisky frescoes by Il Sodoma, p66.

8   San Gimignano A medieval Manhattan perched on a hill, its iconic towers give it the most striking of silhouettes and make it a museum piece in itself, p78.

9   Volterra Indulge your inner archaeologist in Tuscany's wilder west; Etruscan artefacts in the museum and a magnificent Roman theatre, p81.

10   Arezzo Starting point for a Piero della Francesca fest, with frescoes in Arezzo's San Domenico church, and neighbouring Monterchi and Sansepolcro, p91.

Close by is one of the city's oldest churches, Chiesa di San Martino, while in the 15th-century Palazzo Piccolomini, opposite the university, is the city's most unsung treasure – the *Biccherne*, a collection of glorious painted ledgers. This *terzo* is home to the so-called 'unlucky' Contrada della Torre, the tower, which (at the time of writing) hasn't won a Palio for many years. Along Via di Pantaneto are university buildings and a concentration of lively bars and cafés catering for the student population. There are swisher restaurants on adjacent Via del Porrione, from which narrow alleyways lead you to the former Jewish Ghetto – now marked only by the existence of the Synagogue. Streets are often linked by steep flights of steps lending them an air of mystery. Continue walking away from the Campo and you'll reach two of the city gates: Via dei Pispini leads to Porta Pispini, built at the same time as the last ring of city walls; Via Roma leads to Porta Romana, probably the most imposing of all the gates. To reach it you pass the narrow street that leads to the Basilica di Santa Maria dei Servi, a large church with a clutch of paintings and a great view of the city from the top of its steps.

Terzo di Città

Via di Città snakes away from the Campo into this, the oldest of the *terzi*, a tightly meshed labyrinth of backstreets and lanes (*vicoli*); it contains the city's greatest concentration of art treasures. Capillaries, like the Via dei Pellegrini, lead sweating visitors uphill to the Duomo, a dazzling humbug-striped confection that vies for attention with the less glitzy Palazzo Pubblico. Opposite the Duomo is the ancient hospital Santa Maria della Scala, which once treated visiting pilgrims – today tourists on a more prosaic pilgrimage flock inside to see its vibrant frescoes. Via di Città is always busy with shoppers, but cascading down from here are narrow streets that lead to less-visited parts of the city – into the heart of *contrade* like the *Chiocciola* (Snail), the *Pantera* (Panther) and the *Tartuca* (Turtle).

Terzo di Camollia

Covering the area north of the Campo, this *terzo* contains both the oldest and newest buildings in the city. Via Banchi di Sopra, which leads up from the piazza, is the smartest shopping street and throbs with energy as tourists, in trainers and comfy clothes, join cool, effortlessly elegant locals as they prowl the designer stores for classy buys. Continue north and the road morphs into Via di Camollia, where Romanesque churches sit shyly waiting for attention. At the end is the Porta Camollia, the gate that faced the city's great enemy, Florence. The western part of the *terzo* is dominated by the forbidding Medici fortress (its *enoteca* now a lure for wine lovers), by a stretch of public gardens and by the modern football stadium. Trickling east and west of the main artery, narrow streets lead to mighty churches like San Francesco and San Domenico – as well as the ancient home of St Catherine, Siena's beloved patron saint.

Around Siena

One of the delightful things about Siena is that just outside its walls is some of Italy's most stunning countryside – you can see it from many of the city's vantage points. Siena sits in the very heart of Tuscany and the possibilities for exploration are endless. Within an hour you can be in the many-towered hill town of San Gimignano, or sipping a glass of Brunello wine in Montalcino. To the north is Sienese Chianti, the oak-wooded wine country; to the east are Arezzo, Cortona and Sansepolcro, all brimming with fine works of art. And if you want to wander through fields of sunflowers, explore ancient Etruscan cities or just sit in a hilltop village square and watch the world go by, you're just a short drive away.

Trip planner

There's a distinct shortage of accommodation within Siena's walls and you'll need to book well in advance (think about a year) if you want to stay during the Palio (2 July and 16 August). However, high summer outside Palio times can be quieter than you'd expect – largely because it gets extremely hot and uncomfortable for sight-seeing. The other busy spells are around Easter and the months when the floors of the Duomo are on show (generally late August to early October). Spring is a lovely time in Tuscany, ideal for exploring both Siena and the countryside, though be prepared for some rain. October and November are generally cooler, quieter and often surprisingly sunny and, being harvest time, offer the chance to taste fresh *porcini*, truffles and newly pressed olive oil. However, be aware that many hotels and restaurants close for holidays in late November or early December. Winter in Tuscany can be extremely cold, with snow and fog. Visitors should be aware that shops, sights and restaurants generally close on Mondays throughout the year.

24 hours

Siena's definitely worth more than a day, but if you've only got time for a lightning dash it's easy to fit in the main sights as the city's compact and easily explored on foot. Be selective, though: too many frescoes and gilded Madonnas in one day and you won't appreciate any of them. Get up early and wander to the Campo before it fills up, then go into the Palazzo Pubblico to admire the frescoes. If you're feeling energetic you might nip up the Torre del Mangia too, for some great panoramic views over the city. Have a break and relax with a coffee or a *gelato* at one of the cafés on the Campo. After that you could head off down Via del Porrione or Via di Salicotto to explore some of the atmospheric medieval streets, such as Vicolo delle Scotte in the former Jewish quarter. There are plenty of places nearby for lunch, or you could make your way into the Piazza del Mercato where restaurants have lots of outside seats and you get an unusual view of the back of the Palazzo Pubblico. A short walk across the Campo and up Via dei Pellegrini will bring you to the Duomo, where you could easily spend several hours. Make time for Santa Maria della Scala opposite, though, even if you only see the frescoes in the Pilgrims' Hall. Early evening is *passeggiata* time, so join the crowds for some serious shopping and a slug of coffee along Via Banchi di Sopra. Then make your way to one of the many restaurants for dinner. Finish up with a final visit to the Campo, if anything it's even more magical by night.

A long weekend
A weekend in Siena gives you a bit more time to appreciate the main sights as well as to make a leisurely exploration of the maze of steep streets and narrow lanes that so characterize the city. You should certainly visit the Museo dell'Opera del Duomo, both for its artworks and fabulous views from the top. You could fit in a trip to the Pinacoteca if you're a serious art lover, or take a look at the *Biccherne*, the painted book covers in the Palazzo Piccolomini. You'd also have time to take in some historic churches: Sant'Agostino, Basilica di Santa Maria dei Servi and the Basilica di San Francesco should all be high on any itinerary. And of course there's San Domenico church and nearby Casa di Santa Caterina, home of Siena's self-flagellating patron saint. Make time to explore the shops and workshops spread around the city too. A long weekend also gives you the option of having a day out, perhaps taking a bus to San Gimignano or doing a tour of the wine country.

A week or more
A longer break will allow you to spend a few days exploring the sights in the heart of the city, and then head off to enjoy the towns and villages in the surrounding countryside. You would easily have time to explore the stunning landscapes of the Val d'Orcia and Crete Senesi with the hilltop towns of Pienza and Montalcino and the glorious abbey of Monte Oliveto Maggiore. Or you could head north to tour Chianti, go walking around Etruscan Volterra, or make for Arezzo and feast on frescoes by Piero della Francesca.

Contemporary Siena

Proud, passionate, enigmatic, insular – Siena is all of these and more. It is the most complex, fascinating and unfathomable of cities; a place where the medieval is as much a part of modern-day living as the mobile phone. The immaculate condition of its glorious Gothic buildings symbolizes the strength and unity of Sienese society – a society that's tightly bound by the conservative cords of the *contrada* system, which dates back to the Middle Ages. If two Sienese strangers meet, on holiday for example, the first question they'd always ask would be 'What's your *contrada*?' Each *contrada*, or district, is a mix of family, tribe and village; rivalries are fierce, loyalties are strong and every brick of the city is cherished. Visit Siena and you're struck by how clean it is, by the lack of graffiti and by the refreshing absence of police sirens. That's because the *contrade* have strict rules of behaviour and respect, both for the city and one another. Dropping litter, fly hawking of tat for tourists, stealing, taking drugs – none of them are tolerated and consequently Siena is one of the safest cities you could visit.

It's also the most secret of cities. In the same way as a maze of subterranean tunnels silently conveys water to its many fountains, so a hidden life goes on behind its ancient walls and shutters. You could visit a hundred times and never be exposed to it. It's only during the Palio that outsiders really become aware of this inner life. Yet although the Palio is the most important event in Siena, it would mean nothing without the social structures of the *contrada* system. Each *contrada* is a separate community and has its own club, where members socialize away from prying eyes. Traditions are lovingly upheld: when dining, for instance, tables are set separately for men, women and children. The Sienese, considered formal and quiet by other Italians, relax once within their own *contrada*. A lot of time is certainly spent in preparation for the Palio, which constantly occupies people's thoughts. From an early age children are taught skills such as flag waving, and you'll often see them practising in the street. Older people will mend costumes or flags, or prepare food for the victory dinners – everyone has a part to play. But there's more to it than that: if you're in trouble your *contrada* will look after you – you certainly won't get old folk dying alone and neglected in Siena.

Of course any system has its downside and life in such a small community can get claustrophobic at times. And the city itself, with its tight maze of streets, high walls and darkened alleys, can add to that sense of suffocation, creating a sudden need to escape for a while to the fresh green hills that lie just outside its confines. Everyone knows everyone, certainly within a *contrada*, and if you break the unwritten rules you're frozen out. Outsiders say that people can feel under pressure always to look their best and behave in a certain way, though that's hardly unusual in Italy, where presenting a *bella figura* is a matter of national pride. Rivalry between the different *contrade* is generally good humoured and friendly, but tensions can explode during the Palio and fierce fights frequently break out between adversaries. This is the easiest place to understand *Romeo and Juliet*; some Sienese, for instance, would still consider a mixed marriage to be one between members of the rival *contrade*, *Lupa* (Wolf) and *Istrice* (Ostrich). However, it's this rivalry that ironically helps create the remarkable unity of Sienese society.

The close-knit nature of this community can be difficult for outsiders to penetrate and make it hard for them to feel accepted. Other Italians complain that it is impossible ever to be true friends with someone from Siena, and the Sienese say that outsiders can never understand the city or the painful passions of the Palio. In truth they don't really care whether outsiders understand it or not. The term often used is *campanilismo* – literally meaning 'allegiance to one's own belltower'; it implies a provincial, inward-looking and conservative approach to life. Some say it's easier for a foreigner to be accepted here than it is for an Italian from, for example, the surrounding countryside. Schoolchildren always ask newcomers what *contrada* they belong to, and some parents say that children from outside the walls are looked down upon by their peers. However, the real suspicion is directed towards people from Florence, the old enemy to the north. Italy, remember, has only been united since the 19th century. As a visitor, though, you'll find the people courteous, generous and helpful, happy to take time to talk to you and as warmly delighted by a smile or a chubby child as any other Italian.

Siena's an affluent city, with banking, cultural institutions such as the university, and tourism playing an important role in its economy. Important too is agriculture: the surrounding countryside supports a farming community that produces everything from fine honeys to piquant cheese. Local produce is widely used in restaurants and readily available in the small shops that everyone sensibly prefers to supermarkets. It is almost impossible to eat badly here. Appreciation of tradition fills all aspects of life – from the celebration of saints' days to the morning cappuccino – and the Sienese set great store by having a proper lunch, not 'eating at your desk as they do in Milan'. Opening hours aren't written in blood and if the owner of a shop doesn't feel like going in that day or wants to close early, then that's what he or she will do. Traditional crafts are valued and there are lots of ceramic, weaving and other workshops. *Fatto a mano* – made by hand – regularly appears on labels in Sienese shops. Added to the stunning architecture and achingly beautiful countryside, it all makes for an enviable lifestyle. Siena's a flourishing 21st-century medieval city.

Travel essentials

Siena can be reached by air, road and rail. Although it doesn't have a commercial airport, it's easy and cheap to get there from the UK via Tuscany's international gateway, Pisa. From Pisa you can be in Siena in a couple of hours by train, or two and a half hours by bus. Alternatively you can fly to Rome and reach Siena in around three hours by bus.

Once you're in the city, walking is the only option; cars (other than taxis) and bikes are banned, preserving the medieval charm. The advantage to this is you'll be able to justify all those *gelati* in the sure knowledge that you'll soon walk them off again. The city's safe at any time of day or night.

The surrounding countryside is most easily explored by car, especially if you want to tour the hill towns of Chianti or the Val d'Orcia. However, public transport will get you to the main centres, such as San Gimignano. You can also join organized tours; the tourist office and most hotels have details and can book you a place.

Getting there

Air
Alitalia, the Italian state airline, has flights from major cities around the world.

From Europe The most common arrival airport is Pisa (www.pisa-airport.com), connected by direct flights to many European cities including London, Paris, Nice, Frankfurt, Berlin, Hanover, Brussels and Barcelona. Cheapest fares are usually to be found with **Ryanair** which flies from London Stansted and Glasgow Prestwick. Book early and you can find return flights for around £30-50. **British Airways** fly from London Gatwick and Manchester. Return flights around £100.

Less convenient but still a viable option is to fly to Rome. Ryanair fly from London Stansted and London Luton to Rome's Ciampino airport (approx 15 km from central Rome), and **Easy Jet** fly to Ciampino from London Gatwick.

British Airways fly from London Heathrow, Birmingham and Manchester to Rome's Fiumicino (Leonardo da Vinci) airport (32 km from Rome, but with good train links to the city).

Florence airport is gradually increasing its capacity. Airlines providing services to the Florence from European cities include **Air France**, **Austrian**, **Meridiana** and **Lufthansa**. Alitalia provides internal flights from Rome and Milan.

From North America There are no direct flights from North America to Pisa or Florence, but there are direct flights from New York to Rome's main hub, Leonardo da Vinci airport. Airlines include **Alitalia**, **Delta** and **Continental**. Direct flights from other US cities go to Milan, where internal flights link to Pisa. It can also be relatively cheap to fly via London – or another European hub such as Frankfurt or Paris – and connect with flights to Pisa. **Zoom Airlines** fly from Canadian cities to the UK and other European

Airlines

Air France, www.airfrance.com/uk, www.airfrance.fr,
T 0845 0845 111(UK), **T** 1 800 237 2747 (USA)
Alitalia, www.alitalia.it, **T** 0870 608 6001 (UK)
Austrian, www.aua.com, **T** 020 7766 0300 (UK)
British Airways, www.ba.com, **T** 0845 77 333 77 (UK),
T 1 800 247 9297 (USA)
Continental, www.continental.com, **T** 1 800 231 0856 (USA)
Delta, www.delta.com, **T** 1 800 221 1212 (USA)
Easyjet, www.easyjet.com, **T** 0870 6 000 000 (UK)
Lufthansa, www.lufthansa.co.uk, **T** 0845 7737 747 (UK)
Meridiana, www.meridiana.it, **T** 01293 507527 (UK)
Ryanair, www.ryanair.com, **T** 0871 246 0000 (UK),
T 01 609 7800 (Ireland)
Zoom Airlines, www.flyzoom.com, **T** 1 613 235 9666 (Can)

For contact details of airlines in Italy, see p202.

cities. To search for lower-priced flights to Europe from the US, try www.europebyair.com, **T** 888 387 2479.

From Australia and New Zealand There are no direct flights to Italian airports from Australia or New Zealand. You can fly to Rome's Leonardo da Vinci airport via destinations like Singapore, Tokyo or Bankok. Onward connections could also be made through London or other European cities.

Getting to and from the airports Pisa International Airport (Galileo Galilei) is the main international gateway to Tuscany. It's 80 km from Florence. The airport is small and easy to navigate. It has a bank, bureau de change, a cashpoint, shops and a café. There's a tourist information desk and several car hire operators

Discount flight agents

Flight Centre, www.flightcentre.co.uk, **T** 0870 4990040 (UK)
STA Travel, www.statravel.co.uk, **T** 0870 1600 599 (UK)
Trailfinders, www.trailfinders.com, **T** 0845 058 5858 (UK)
Travel Cuts, www.travelcuts.com, **T** 1 866 246 9762 (Can/USA)

Online operators

www.avro.com
www.cheapflights.co.uk
www.easyvalue.com
www.ebookers.com
www.expedia.co.uk, www.expedia.com
www.lastminute.com
www.opodo.com
www.travelocity.com

including **Avis**, **Europcar**, **Liberty Rent International**,
Maggiore and **Sixt Rent a Car**. There is a ticket office that sells
both train and bus tickets to Florence.

The quickest way to reach Siena is by **train** (price €6.50). The
station is beside the airport, to the left of the exit. Trains usually
leave hourly from 0900 or 1000, to 1900. You can get regular trains
to Empoli (sometimes direct, sometimes via **Pisa Centrale**, a five-
minute ride away) where you change for Siena. Siena station is
about 2 km outside the historical centre – taxis are available
outside; otherwise you can get a bus, though these go only to the
northern part of the city.

You can also go by train to Florence's **Santa Maria Novella**
station (€5) where you take the right-hand exit for the **SITA**
bus station, about two minutes' walk away, between Via
Alamani and Via della Scala. Blue SITA buses leave from here

to Siena (€6.50). Tickets are available from the office inside the bus station. Buses leave approximately every 30 minutes and the efficient non-stop service takes one hour 15 minutes. Buses run from around 0645 to 2015. There's also a service via Colle di Val d'Elsa that takes a bit longer. The advantage of the bus is that it delivers you to the centre of Siena, to the bus station at Piazza Gramsci.

A **Terravision shuttle bus** goes from Pisa Airport to Florence Santa Maria Novella station. It runs daily from around 0830 to 2230 and links up to Ryanair flights. It takes about one hour 10 minutes and tickets cost from €4.90 single (€10.50 at peak times). Buses stop outside the station and it's just a short walk to the SITA bus station and connections to Siena.

From **Rome Fiumicino** (Leonardo da Vinci) airport get a shuttle train to central Rome (every 15 minutes). You can then get a bus or train to Siena. To get the bus, go to Rome's **Tiburtina** station where a SENA bus goes to Siena (3½ hours, €17.50-€20.50 if you get the ticket on board). For the train, get off at Rome's Termini station. Trains go to Chiusi, where you change for Siena (approximately 3½ hours, €12.34).

From **Rome Ciampino** airport **Terravision** buses go to Rome's **Termini** station. They connect with Ryanair flights and the journey costs €8.

From **Florence (Amerigo Vespucci)** airport a **Vola in Bus** (Fly by Bus, www.ataf.net) shuttle service leaves approximately every half hour for **Santa Maria Novella** station. Journey takes around 30 minutes and costs €4. You would then catch the SITA bus to Siena.

Road

Car Italy has a good network of *autostrade* (motorways), the main north-south link being the A1. **From Florence** take the Firenze Certosa exit off the ring road, then join the SS2 *superstrada* to Siena. Exit at Siena Pta San Marco and follow signs for centre and parking at La Fortezza. (approximately one hour). **From Rome** take the A1 direction Florence, exit at Valdichiana, then turn right on route 326 – Siena. Take the Siena Sud by-pass, direction Florence, exit at Siena Pta San Marco for parking at La Fortezza. (approximately three hours).

All motorways are tolled, but the dual carriageway *strade statali* 'SS' roads are not. Speed limits on motorway are (nominally anyway) 130 kmph (81 mph) for cars of 110cc or more and 110 kmph (68 mph) for smaller cars. The lower limit applies to all cars on SS roads.

EU nationals taking their own car need an International Insurance Certificate or Green Card – **Carta Verde**. Those without an EU licence need an International Driving Permit. **Autostrade (T** 055 420 3200, www.autostrade.it) provides information on motorways in Italy, and **Automobile Club Italiana** – ACI – (**T** 06 49981 or 4477 for 24-hour information) provides general driving information.

Coach Should you wish to put yourself through it, you can reach Siena by coach from London. You'll leave Victoria coach station about 0800 and reach Florence in about 29 hours (£69 to £139). Once in Florence you take the bus to Siena. Contact **National Express Eurolines T** 08705 143219, www.eurolines.co.uk.

Train
Siena is on a provincial railway line, so the main connecting station for international rail travellers is **Florence Santa Maria Novella** (www.firenzesantamarianovella.it). This station has a café/bar, pharmacy, newsagents, post office, left luggage and supermarket. It's possible to travel from the UK by **Eurostar** (**T** 08705 186186, www.eurostar.com, or through Rail Europe, **T** 08708 371371, www.raileurope.co.uk). Trains leave Waterloo International for Paris (usually Gard du Nord). Ticket prices vary from around £59, for a return ticket – rising to

nearly £200. Change in Paris to Gare de Bercy where a train leaves at around 1900 arriving at Santa Maria Novella at around 0730 the next morning (approximately £74).

Florence has direct links to other European cities (eg Basel and Munich). It is also connected to Italian cities such as Bologna (one hour), Venice (two hours 50 minutes), Milan (approximately three hours 20 minutes), and Rome (three hours). The Italian State Railway **Trenitalia** (www.trenitalia.com) runs an efficient service and fares are excellent value, some of the best in Europe. A ticket isn't valid until it has been stamped in one of the yellow boxes on the platform. Most trains only require a standard ticket, but some express trains such as **Intercity** require a supplement, and sometimes a reservation. A **Trenitalia Pass**, available for visitors, covers all rail travel in Italy for a fixed period. There are different categories lasting from four to ten days and they cost from €217 to €349.

Getting around

Bike
Bikes are banned from virtually the whole of the historic centre. If you want to explore the surrounding countryside you can hire bikes from **Walking and Cycling Agency**, and other agencies in town (see Cycling, p191, and Bicycle hire, p202). Ask at the tourist office for a copy of the brochure *Terre di Siena in Bici*, which gives suggested itineraries (www.terresiena.it).

Bus
Although Siena is pedestrianized, there's a small bus **Pollicino** (run by Tra.in www.trainspa.it) which covers a few streets in the centre.

Siena's main bus station is on Piazza Gramsci, although some buses leave from the train station. Information is available at the centre in the underpass, below the piazza. The main companies are **SITA** (www.sita-on-line.it) and **Tra.in** and they run services to towns and villages around Siena. There's a regular service to Colle di Val d'Esla, San Gimignano and Arezzo. Less frequent buses go to the main Chianti towns and to Montepulciano and San Quirico d'Orcia. Purchase tickets at the bus station, or from *tabacchi* (tobacconists). Tickets need to be validated at the machine on board. A return to San Quirico, for example, costs €6.

Car
Cars are banned from the centre – part of its charm is that it's virtually traffic free. Car parks are located on the outskirts (there's a large one by the Fortezza). Some hotels have parking for guests. For information contact **Siena Parcheggi**, **T** 0577 228711.

Taxi
Taxis are expensive and you will be charged extra for each item of luggage. There's a taxi rank on Piazza Matteotti and one by the station. To call a taxi **T** 0577 49222, or 44504.

Train
Trains run regularly to Arezzo, where connecting trains go to Camucia, the nearest station to Cortona. They are cheap and generally efficient. For information, go to www.trenitalia.it.

Walking
Siena is small enough to explore on foot – which is handy because the historic centre is pedestrian only. It's compact, but get a good map as you can easily get lost in the medieval maze. Some streets are extremely steep.

Museum passes

Itinerari d'arte ticket is a combination ticket giving entrance to the Museo Civico, Santa Maria della Scala, Museo dell'Opera del Duomo, Battistero, Chiesa Sant'Agostino, and the Oratorio di San Bernardino. It is valid for seven days, costs €16, and is available from the Tourist Office.
Musei Comunali ticket covers joint entry to the Museo Civico and Santa Maria della Scala. It is valid for two days and costs €10.

Tours

Walking tours
Giorgia Scarpelli, **T** 0577 223039, **T** 335 432972 (mob), giorgia.scarpelli@libero.it, or through Guide Siena (see below). Excellent guide to Siena city, particularly knowledgeable on art history.

Guide Siena, **T** 0577 43273, www.guidesiena.it. They organize a *Siena by Night* walking tour that meets at 2130 on Tuesday and Friday in the Campo.

Tours outside Siena
Siena Point, Via della Sapienza, **T** 0577 222684, www.sienapoint.com. A wide range of tours from hot-air ballooning, to tours of San Gimignano, Volterra, Chianti and the Val d'Orcia. You can also rent a smart car from them.

Tuscan Tour, **T** 347 143 5004, www.tuscantour.com. Good guided tours of Tuscan cities, by a knowledgeable and helpful guide.

Il Casato, Via Casato di Sotto, **T** 0577 46091, www.siena holiday.com. For wine tours and visits to Monte Oliveto Maggiore.

Train tours
The **Nature Train** runs vintage diesel and steam trains from Siena to Monte Amiata. It's seasonal and dates should be checked beforehand. It's a circular route through the Val d'Orcia and Crete Senese. No booking is needed for diesel trips (it is for steam journeys) and tickets can be bought on board. Round trips €15. **Val d'Orcia Railway**, **T** 0577 207413, www.ferrovieturistiche.it.

Tourist information

Siena Tourist Board, Piazza del Campo, **T** 0577 280551, www.terresiena.it, www.siena.turismo.toscana.it. *Daily 0830-1930*. Main tourist office, will book hotels, have a selection of leaflets and information on tours and attractions. Also look at the website of the town council, www.comune.siena.it.

Most towns and villages have their own tourist offices. These are the major ones:

Arezzo, Piazza della Repubblica 28, **T** 0575 20839, www.apt.arezzo.it.

Castellina in Chianti, Via Ferruccio 40, **T** 0577 741392, info@essenceoftuscany.it.

Cortona, Via Nazionale 42, **T** 0575 630352, infocortona@apt.arezzo.it.

Montalcino, Costa del Municipio 8, **T** 0577 849331, www.prolocomontalcino.it.

Pienza, Corso Rossellino 59, **T** 0578 749071,
www.communedipienza.it.

San Gimignano, Piazza del Duomo 1, **T** 0577 940008,
www.sangimignano.com.

San Quirico d'Orcia, Via Dante Alighieri 33, **T** 0577 898303,
www.parcodellavaldorcia.com.

Volterra, Piazza dei Priori 19-20, **T** 0588 87257, www.volterratur.it.

Piazza del Campo and around 31

The dramatic shell-shaped piazza that links
the *terzi*, the thirds, or districts into which
the city has traditionally been divided. Home
of the magnificent Palazzo Pubblico and its
ancient tower.

Terzo di San Martino 37

The southeast *terzo* that leads to the imposing
Porta Romana. It holds most of the city's
Renaissance buildings, a clutch of fine restaurants
and some funky bars.

Terzo di Città 42

The oldest district and tourist hub. The ancient
heart of Siena where the cathedral and pilgrims'
hospital perch above a maze of darkened lanes.

Terzo di Camollia 53

Urban buzz, the sassiest shops, focus of the
evening *passeggiata*, a glowering fortress and
the home of a saint.

Piazza del Campo and around

All life in Siena converges on Il Campo, the scallop-shaped piazza that's the heart of the city and links the terzi, or thirds, into which the city is divided. It's a magical medieval amphitheatre, paved in rosy-red bricks sloping gently towards the Palazzo Pubblico. It's the first stop for cone-licking day trippers and the natural gathering place for locals and visitors. The Campo's enclosed by a towering ring of ancient palaces which give it an insular atmosphere all of its own – and keep its splendour a secret until the last minute. Neutral territory, not belonging to any contrada, it's the setting for the Palio (p170) and practically bulges when crowds pour in to watch the race. Once the forum of the Roman settlement Sena Julia, it was designed in the Middle Ages by the Council of Nine, the city's rulers from 1287-1355. It was in their honour that the piazza was divided into nine segments by marble strips. Today it's encircled with cafés and bars. Yet although it sizzles with people during the day, at night it becomes surprisingly hushed, the darkness giving it a slightly eerie quality.

▸▸ *See Eating and drinking p125, Bars and clubs p155*

◉ Sights

Il Campo
Map 2, B5, p236

The Campo – the name means 'field', was completed in the 1340s. In medieval times all manner of activities took place here: bullfights, boxing matches, the Palio, trading – even executions. The design was carefully planned. In 1297, the authorities decreed that the frontages of any buildings should harmonize with the Palazzo Pubblico, the seat of government, and although alterations have taken place over the years the impression is still remarkably medieval. The Campo is home to the **Fonte Gaia**, 'fountain of joy', a favourite photo-stop with visitors. It's a 19th-century copy of the original fountain, by Jacopo della Quercia in 1419. A deep pool surrounded by reliefs of Adam, Eve and allegorical figures, it was intended to be a key feature of the Renaissance in Siena, rivalling Florence's celebrated Baptistry doors by Ghiberti. The original fountain is now displayed in the Spedale di Santa Maria della Scala (p49).

A statue of Venus once sat on top of the Fonte Gaia. However, after the Black Death, religious leaders said God was punishing the Sienese for displaying this pagan statue. Venus was promptly destroyed. But they didn't let the pieces go to waste – they buried them in Florentine territory, hoping to pass the curse to their enemy.

★ Palazzo Pubblico and Museo Civico

Piazza del Campo, **T** 0577 292263, www.comune.siena.it/museocivico. *Winter 1000-1730 (approx), summer 1000-1900. €7; joint ticket with Santa Maria della Scala €10. Map 2, B5, p236*

Occupying almost the whole of the south side of the Campo, the Palazzo Pubblico is a monumental Gothic building, constructed in the late 13th century as the seat of the Sienese government. It was built to impress – a symbol of the city's independence and power – and still succeeds. Today, as well as being the home of the city authorities, it houses the Museo Civico, a series of frescoed rooms and grand halls that reflect medieval life.

The first few rooms contain a jumble of paintings from the 16th to 18th centuries. If you're short of time skip them to reach the **Sala del Risorgimento**, covered in colourful 19th-century frescoes celebrating the unification of Italy and Vittorio Emanuele II, the first king. Scenes include his meeting with Garibaldi and allegorical depictions of Italy.

! According to Will Self, the Palazzo Pubblico is "the finest example of 14th-century vernacular architecture in the known world" (*Independent*, 2004).

It is like a bit of Venice, without the water.

Charles Dickens on Siena (Pictures from Italy, 1846)

Turn left out of here to climb the stairs to the **Loggia**, a wide terrace built for the Council of Nine (see p211) so that they could get some fresh air during the months when they were unable to leave the palace. There are great views to the surrounding countryside.

Back downstairs is the **Anticamera del Concistoro**, with a fragment of a fresco attributed to Ambrogio Lorenzetti. This leads to the **Anticappella**, decorated with frescoes by Taddeo di Bartolo, and the **Cappella** (chapel), surrounded by a strikingly elaborate wrought-iron screen by Jacopo della Quercia. Every inch of the chapel is covered with frescoes. One of the most important works is Il Sodoma's (p73) altarpiece of *La Sacra Famiglia con San Leonardo* (*Holy Family with St Leonard*), painted around 1530. But spare some time for the 22 inlaid wooden choir stalls too, carved by Domenico di Niccolò. They're said to be the first example of conceptual art.

Look at the basin for holy water by the chapel entrance. There's a small metal ring beside it into which single Sienese girls have traditionally inserted their ring fingers hoping it will bring them a husband. Look closely on the opposite wall and you can see medieval graffiti.

One of the most important rooms in the palace is the richly decorated **Sala del Mappamondo**, once used as the law court and named after a rotating wheel map of the world, painted by Ambrogio Lorenzetti, *c*1344. Now all that remains are the marks where it was fixed to the wall. Above this is the fresco of *Guidoriccio da Fogliano all'Assedio di Montemassi* (*Guidoriccio da Fogliano at the Siege of Montemassi*) in which da Fogliano, a Sienese army leader and his horse – both draped in golden cloth – ride across newly conquered territories, dotted with castles and tents. Dated 1328 it was attributed to Simone Martini, although some now doubt this, saying that the style of castle points to it being a 16th-century fake; others believe it's genuine and was simply restored by later artists. Beneath this is a newly revealed fresco of two men engaged in the purchase of a fenced castle. The oldest fresco in the palace, it had been covered with plaster for years. Recent studies attribute it to Duccio di Buoninsegna.

Opposite is one of Simone Martini's finest works, the *Maestà* (1315) in which Mary sits on a gilded throne under a canopy supported by apostles, rather as if she's attending a medieval tournament. It was the first in Siena to show Mary on a sky blue, rather than regal gold, background, making her much more human. The picture – one of the most important in Siena – symbolizes the ideal of a good and just governor and was a reminder for leaders to govern fairly and not take advantage of their power. On the beams above the *Maestà* you can see a hand peeping out on either side. These would once have held curtains that framed the painting.

The **Sala della Pace**, the meeting room of the Council of Nine (see p211), contains some of Europe's most important medieval secular frescoes: the *Allegories of Good and Bad Government*. Painted by Ambrogio Lorenzetti between 1337 and 1339, they were commissioned by the remarkably enlightened Council of Nine as a constant reminder of the need to use their power wisely. On one wall a bearded *Good Government* sits enthroned, attended by figures including Justice, Wisdom and Charity. Beside them, a vibrant panorama shows the effect it would have on the city – Siena as observed by Lorenzetti from the palace windows. You can see contented citizens going about their business, while masons construct new buildings. Outside, by the Porta Romana, a well-dressed party of falconers ride their horses into safe and fertile countryside. You can even spot a man leading a distinctive black and white Sienese pig. On the other wall *Bad Government* is represented by a devil, aided by Vice who has unceremoniously squashed Justice. The effects are dramatic and the accompanying panorama depicts a threatening landscape – dry, bare and full of robbers; the city is ruined and violence reigns. The message is clear: behave, or else.

Tunnel vision

Unlike many major cities, Siena is not built on a river and has no natural water supply. It needed one to grow successfully, but the Sienese didn't want to built aqueducts – their enemies could have sabotaged them too easily. Instead they built tunnels, *bottini*, which channelled water from the distant hills to large fountains in the city. The water was so precious that the fountains were under 24-hour armed guard. Work began in the 13th century and continued for 200 years – the network covers 24 km. The medieval workmen had only basic equipment but were highly skilled; the tunnels still work efficiently. Ironically, they also provided an efficient method of spreading the plague, which ravaged the city in the 14th century. Visits to the *bottini* are hard to arrange and must be booked well in advance. Information from the Associazione La Diana, www.comune.siena.it/diana/

Torre del Mangia

Palazzo Pubblico, Piazza del Campo. *Winter 1000-1600 (approx), summer 1000-1900 (approx).* €6; joint ticket with museum €10; closed for safety reasons if raining. Tickets can be pre-booked. Map 2, B5, p236 See also p197

Turn left when you enter the palace to climb the thigh-tightening, 388 steps of this 102-m tower, which gives outstanding views of the city. Topped with an enormous bell, it once dominated the Sienese skyline, a symbol of the Republic's authority over any competing religious and aristocratic powers. It gets its name from one of the first bellringers, a lazy, fat man nicknamed *Mangiaguadagni* – 'eat the profits'.

Terzo di San Martino

The Terzo di San Martino runs from the Campo to the southeast corner of the city and contains most of the city's Renaissance buildings. University buildings and language schools are here and consequently there are plenty of lively bars, internet cafés and good-value eateries catering for the students. It's also a great place to wander off the tourist track and soak up the atmosphere of some of Siena's most atmospheric viccoli – the darkened narrow lanes that so characterize the city.

▸▸ *See Sleeping p103, Eating and drinking p126, Bars and clubs p155*

★ Palazzo Piccolomini and Museo delle Tavolette di Biccherna

Via Banchi di Sotto 52. *Guided tours Mon-Sat 0930, 1030, 1130 only. Free. Entrance is across the square in the palazzo through the door on the left. Map 2, A6, p236*

Most visitors bypass this 14th-century palace, which houses the dull-sounding state archives. Yet they're missing a treasure, an unusual collection of over 100 beautifully illustrated ledgers. The *Biccherne*, as they're known, are decorated wooden covers that protected the city's accounting sheets. The first was commissioned in 1257 and they were produced until the 17th century. The finest Sienese artists were entrusted with this work (including Ambrogio Lorenzetti, Sano di Pietro and Benvenuto di Giovanni) and the resultant paintings are little masterpieces. What's most interesting is the subject matter – the daily life of the city. The earliest show monastic treasurers counting money, a man washing his hands, a wedding and the Duomo. The *Biccherne* gradually became more sophisticated, depicting significant events in Siena such as the *terremoto* (earthquake) of 1467. Historical events were also recalled, such as the coronation of Pope Pius II in 1460, or the Spanish destroying the walls of Siena. Over time they became paintings, hung on the office walls, rather than covering books. They grew in size but lacked the integrity of the earliest works.

The archive also houses illuminated manuscripts, 60,000 scrolls and thousands of books. Opposite is a small museum belonging to the university.

Via di Pantaneto and around
Map 2, B9, p237

At the top of Via di Pantaneto – the name comes from *pantano* the old local word for mud or bog – is the **Logge del Papa**, a striking white loggia. Commissioned by Pope Pius II (p71), it is the most important Renaissance monument in Siena and was designed in 1462 by Antonio Federighi. To the right of it, on Via del Porrione, is **Chiesa di San Martino** (*0930-1230, 1800-1900*). Despite its 17th-century façade, this is one of the oldest churches in the city, though it has been altered many times over the years. The high altar is adorned with marble angels and there's a 16th-century painting of the *Madonna* protecting the city. Via di Pantaneto is lined with old palaces such as the 15th-century **Palazzo di San Galgano**. Today it's the heart of student Siena, and is filled with bars, cafés, internet cafés and laundries. It runs down into Via Roma, at the bottom of which is the **Porta Romana**, the most imposing gate in the city walls. Completed around 1330, it was later decorated with a fresco (now gone) by Sienese painter Sassetta (1394-1450) who became ill while carrying out the work; the illness killed him.

● *Linking Via di Pantaneto and Via del Porrione is an atmospheric little lane called Vicolo delle Scotte. Once part of the Jewish Ghetto it's home to the Synagogue, built in the late 18th century. The Jewish community is now very small but you can visit the Synagogue (T 055 234 6654, Sun 1000-1300, 1400-1700 approx, guided tours only, book ahead).*

Basilica di Santa Maria dei Servi

Piazza Alessandro Manzoni. *0830-1230, 1530-1830. Free.*
Map 2, F11, p237

Down near the Porta Romana is this enormous church, one of
Siena's most significant. Building began in 1235, but continued
until well after it was consecrated in 1533 and the façade was
never completed. From outside you have a lovely view of the city.
Inside it's wide and airy, supported by rows of columns, and with
side chapels containing many important paintings. To the right of
the entrance is *Our Lady with Child and Two Angels*, painted in 1261
by Coppo di Marcovaldo. A Florentine artist, he was taken prisoner
in the Battle of Montaperti (p56) by the Sienese, who then
cunningly demanded that he paint this picture in return for his
freedom. Other works include two gruesome versions of *The
Slaughter of the Innocents*, one by Matteo di Giovanni (c1430-1497)
and another by Pietro Lorenzetti (c1280-1348), and a fresco of *The
Banquet of Herod* also by Pietro Lorenzetti.

Convento di San Girolamo

Piazzetta San Girolamo. *Mon-Sat during the day. Off Via dei Servi.*
Map 2, E10, p237

Not far from the Basilica di Santa Maria dei Servi, this little convent
dates back to 1470. Ring the bell, and once she's peeped at you
through the window, a nun will let you in. The lavish church
contains Francesco Vanni's painting of *Santa Caterina drinking the
blood of Christ*, and an *Annunciation* by Rutilio Manetti. In an alcove
in the passage outside is a vibrant fresco by Fungari.

The contrade

Siena is split into 17 *contrade*, legally chartered districts which function almost as villages within the city and date back at least as far as the 13th century. There were originally many more of them but by the 17th century some had merged. They grew up when Siena was a free state, and had duties such as collecting taxes and maintaining fountains. They also each had to send a force to defend Siena if under attack. Now they have powers rather like local authorities.

You're born into a *contrada* and can't change it. Each one has its own traditions, church, museum, bar and club, symbol, colours and fountain. Keep your eyes peeled and you'll see symbols on streets indicating which *contrada* you're in. Every week members of the *contrada*, *contradaioli*, gather for dinners; it's like a large family and loyalties are fierce. Babies in Siena are baptized twice: into the church and into the *contrada*, where they're given their *fazzoletto*, *contrada* scarf. So strong are the bonds that many men wear gold rings on the third finger of their right hands, leading to comments that they're married to their *contrada* rather than their wife.

For historical reasons, most of which are long forgotten, most Contrade have an enemy. Many Sienese like to wear the colours of their own district, and certainly wouldn't wear those of their enemy. Peep into the windows of houses and you might well see *contrada* symbols dotted around (ceramic geese say, or model snails). However, only tourists buy the ceramics decorated with all the different Contrade symbols; the Sienese wouldn't dream of it.

Every year 10 of the 17 take part in the Palio (p170), and open-air dinners are held not only to celebrate their victories, but also to celebrate their enemy's losses. Yet although most attention is focused on the Palio, it's just the tip of the iceberg; it's the *contrada* system itself that keeps Siena going. There's an unwritten code of behaviour and if you don't observe it you're frozen out.

Very occasionally the Contrade museums and churches are opened to the public. Otherwise, if you want to see them, you'll have to ring and arrange a visit (p203).

Contrasting the contrade

Each *contrada* has its own symbol, its own colours and, with a few exceptions, its own traditional enemy:

Terzo di San Martino

Civetta (Owl); enemy *Leocorno*; maroon, black and a dash of white.
Leocorno (Unicorn), enemy *Civetta*; orange, white and blue.
Nicchio (Shell); enemy *Valdimontone*; bright blue with a little yellow and red.
Valdimontone (Ram); enemy *Nicchio*; scarlet, yellow and a little white.
Torre (Tower, often an elephant with a tower on its back); enemy *Oca* and *Onda*; dark red with a little white and pale blue. Considered an 'unlucky' *contrada* as it has hardly won any Palios.

Terzo di Città

Aquila (Eagle), enemy *Pantera*; yellow and black.
Chiocciola (Snail); enemy *Tartuca*; red, yellow and blue.
Onda (Wave, symbolized by a dolphin); enemy *Torre*; blue and white.
Pantera (Panther); enemy *Aquila*; blue, red and white.
Selva (Woodland, symbolized by a rhino under a tree); no enemy, orange, white and green.
Tartuca (Turtle); enemy *Chiocciola*; blue and yellow.

Terzo di Camollia

Bruco (Caterpillar); no enemy, yellow and green.
Drago (Dragon); no enemy; green, deep pink and yellow.
Giraffa (Giraffe); no enemy, red and white.
Istrice (Porcupine); enemy *Lupa*; light red, black, blue and white.
Lupa (She-wolf); enemy *Istrice*; white, black and a little orange.
Oca (Goose); enemy *Torre*; green and white with a little orange. St Catherine was born into the Contrada dell'Oca, which has won many Palios; they claim they have a 'friend in heaven'.

For contact details of the *contrade* headquarters, see p203.

Terzo di Città

This is Siena's oldest district. The ancient town stood on its highest point, tightly knit around a castle – the area eventually became known as Castelvecchio and there's still a street of that name. It was here, on a site once used for pagan worship, that the earliest church was built – the forerunner of the Duomo (cathedral). The Duomo, with its distinctive stripes, is now one of Siena's main attractions and queues of visitors frequently snake down its steps and onto the piazza as they wait to file inside. There's enough there to occupy you for the best part of a day. Most of the city's finest works of art are squeezed into this terzo's *twisting streets: not just in the Duomo, but also in the Spedale di Santa Maria della Scala, the former hospital that's been converted into a museum, and in the Pinacoteca Nazionale, the art gallery that holds a precious collection of Sienese paintings. The main street, Via di Città, links the district to the Campo. It's lined with shops, many selling ceramics aimed at tourists but others offering high-quality crafts and handmade clothes. It's generally crowded with visitors – who frequently fail to explore the atmospheric alleys that lurk nearby.*

▸▸ *See Sleeping p104, Eating and drinking p129, Bars and clubs p156*

★ Duomo

Piazza del Duomo, off Via di Città, **T** 0577 283048, www.operaduomo.siena.it. *Mar-Oct Mon-Sat 1030-1930, Sun 1330-1930; Nov-Mar Mon-Sat 1030-1830, Sun 1330-1730. €6 when floor is uncovered (late Aug-early Oct, dates vary), otherwise free. Piccolomini Library €3 . Map 2, C2, p236*

The Duomo (cathedral) justifies the term 'jaw-dropping'. Consecrated in 1179, it continued to grow over the years, becoming increasingly ornate in the process. Early visitors on the Grand Tour found it stunning – and sometimes shocking: John Ruskin, who had a headache at the time, described it as "absurd… a piece of costly confectionery".

★ Best

Places to see frescoes

- Palazzo Pubblico, p32
- Cripta di San Giovanni, p46
- Santa Maria della Scala, p49
- San Francesco Church, Arezzo, p91
- Madonna del Parto, Monterchi, p94

The lower part of the **façade** was lavishly carved by Giovanni Pisano in the late 13th century and although his original statues have now been moved to the Museo dell'Opera del Duomo (p45) to protect them, the copies that replace them mean that none of the effect is lost. The upper half of the façade was begun later and the mosaics at the top weren't added until the 19th century. The humbug-striped bell tower was built around 1313.

The Duomo was meant to be even larger. Early in the 14th century the Sienese decided to make their cathedral the largest in Christendom. But work had to be abandoned when the Black Death of 1348 decimated the population and sparked an economic crisis. The Museo dell'Opera del Duomo is now housed in what would have been the right nave, and the frame of the façade is nearby.

The interior is visually stunning and surprisingly colourful; it's hard to know where to look first. Shaped like a Latin cross, there are three enormous aisles. The columns and walls are covered with black and white zebra stripes; the ceiling and arches are decorated too; faces of 172 former popes peer down at you from on high and the **floor**, or *pavimento* as it's known, is covered with 56 *sgraffito* marble squares. Work on these began in 1367 and continued for 200 years, involving many of Siena's finest artists such as Pinturicchio, Beccafumi and Matteo di Giovanni. In black and white with touches of yellow and red, these magnificent mosaics tell stories from the Old Testament and from mythology. They include the Sienese she-wolf surrounded by an elephant, lion and a unicorn, and are extremely detailed. Look closely and you'll see carefully crafted snails, frogs and tortoises. In order to preserve it, most of the floor is covered except from late August to around early October (dates vary).

The **Piccolomini Library**, off the left aisle, is like a jewel box. It was built in 1495 to celebrate the life of Pope Pius II on the orders of his nephew, Cardinal Francesco Piccolomini – later Pius III. The lower part is lined with cases containing illuminated manuscripts of Gregorian chants. The walls are covered with frescoes depicting 10 important scenes in the life of this humanist pope – born Enea (sometimes spelled Aeneas) Silvius de' Piccolomini (p71). They were painted by Pinturicchio in the early 16th century and are characteristically richly coloured. Among the frescoes are Enea, then an envoy, attending the court of James II of Scotland, with a most unlikely – and hot-looking – exotic landscape in the background. Other scenes show him being crowned poet laureate, becoming pope and canonizing St Catherine of Siena. The last panel shows his death.

To the left of the library is the Piccolomini altar with statues of saints. Most are by Michelangelo but one, *St Francis*, is by Torrigiani, who gained notoriety for breaking Michelangelo's nose in a fit of jealousy. By the chapel of San Giovanni Battista, is a bronze statue of *St John the Baptist* in rags, by Donatello (1457), and the tomb of Cardinal Riccardo Petroni, by Sienese artist Tino di Camaino. On the left, behind the altar are inlaid choir stalls, showing life-like birds, streets and buildings.

The marble **pulpit** is a masterpiece, sculpted by Nicola Pisano (father of Giovanni Pisano who carved the façade) between 1265 and 1268. He was the first 'modern' sculptor in Italy, giving emotion to his subjects. The figure of Christ on the cross is portrayed as a suffering man rather than a triumphant divine figure. There are 300 human figures on the pulpit, and all the faces are different. Look at the columns here. At one point the zebra stripes become much more widely spaced. This indicates an early extension to the original cathedral.

The **Cappella della Madonna del Voto**, was designed by Bernini, adorned with lapis lazuli, and contains a medieval picture of the Virgin, said to grant miracles. Hanging beside it are all sorts of offerings. They range from cycle helmets and baby shoes to *contrade* scarves and horses' bits – the latter giving thanks for 'miraculous' Palio victories.

★ Museo dell'Opera del Duomo

Piazza della Quercia, **T** 0577 283048, www.operaduomo.siena.it. *By the Duomo. Mid Mar-end Sept 0900-1930, Oct 0900-1800, Nov-mid Mar 0900-1330. €6. Map 2, C3, p236*

Occupying what was intended to be the nave of the extended Duomo, this museum houses much of the Duomo's art collection. Among the works are the original sculptures from the façade and, most famous of all, Duccio's *Maestà*.

The tour starts upstairs where you can see icons and altarpieces, including a Byzantine work, *Madonna degli Occhi Grossi*, 'of the Big Eyes', which was painted early in the 13th century and was the cathedral's original altarpiece. The Sienese prayed in front of it to ask the Virgin for protection before the Battle of Montaperti (p56). They won and the Virgin became their patron saint.

The most important room is the **Sala il Duccio**, which contains Duccio di Buoninsegna's masterly *Maestà*, a double-sided work which was painted on wood for the Duomo's high altar. It took three years to paint. Completed in 1311, it was carried ceremoniously from his workshop to the cathedral attended by virtually everyone in the city. It is richly gilded and depicts the *Madonna and Child* on a marble throne, surrounded by saints and angels, and is considered one of the most important paintings in medieval art. The back is covered with scenes depicting the *Passion of Christ*. Drawing on Byzantine tradition mingled with lyrical elements of humanity and narrative, it essentially founded the Sienese school of painting. Not all the panels are here, as some are in foreign museums.

Other works include Duccio's *Madonna di Crevole* (1283) and Pietro Lorenzetti's *Birth of the Virgin*. The lower floor is dedicated to statues, including those carved by Giovanni Pisano that would once have covered the façade of the Duomo. The figures seem to loom over you, fingers raised, sizing you up with unseeing eyes. You leave the museum through the high baroque church of **San Niccolò in Sasso**, adorned with lavish stucco work and an inlaid floor.

● *Make sure you follow the signs to the **Panorama dal Facciatone**, where narrow spiral stairs lead up onto the walls of the abandoned extension – vertigo sufferers might want to avoid the very exposed top level, but the view really is worth the climb.*

Cripta di San Giovanni

Piazza della Quercia, **T** 0577 283048, www.operaduomo.siena.it. *Mid Mar-late Sep 0900-1930, Oct 0900-1800, Nov-mid Mar 0900-1330. €6. Map 2, C3, p236*

Tucked behind the back of the Duomo and the top of the steps leading down to the Baptistry, it would be easy to miss this little treasure. The term crypt is a misnomer, since it was more probably a hall leading to the pilgrims' entrance to the Duomo. Having followed the Via Francigena tired, hungry pilgrims would first enter this hall to prepare themselves for their devotions. Here they could wash, purify themselves and have something to eat before going into the Duomo. However, it was filled with rubble and sealed up when the Baptistry was built, and was only rediscovered in 1999 by a workman swinging a pickaxe. The walls are covered with brilliantly coloured, and perfectly preserved 13th- and 14th-century frescoes depicting stories of the Old and New Testament. Among the artists involved were Guido and Renaldo da Siena and Guido di Graziano. On the

The Golden Age

Gilded paintings of the Madonna characterize Sienese art. The Virgin Mary had been important here from early medieval times. The citizens believed she was their protector and had been responsible for their victory at the Battle of Montaperti (p56), so sparking a production line of paintings. A Florentine artist, Coppo di Marcovaldo, had been taken prisoner at Montaperti and the Sienese demanded a painting as a ransom. It took him a year to do (you can see it in the Basilica di Santa Maria dei Servi) and during that time he met and influenced local artist Guido da Siena. Up to then, Sienese artists – always more conservative than those in Florence – had followed the Romanesque tradition, which had strong Byzantine roots. Figures were flat, with emphasis on their eyes and hands and, rather than natural settings, artists used gold leaf for backgrounds – suggesting that their subjects were bathed in divine light. Guido began to relax this rigidity. He was followed by Duccio di Buoninsegna, the acknowledged father of the Sienese School. Duccio skilfully combined Byzantine tradition with Northern European, Gothic influences. He produced a new painting of the Madonna and Child, his *Maestà*, for the high altar of the Duomo. Although it still has the typically Byzantine gilding, there's more movement: faces turn in various directions, it's not so flat, and Christ is more childlike. Duccio's pupil, Simone Martini, introduced an even more relaxed Gothic style and gave a human dimension to his religious subjects. More emotional works followed with the Lorenzetti brothers, the latter painting the political frescoes in the Palazzo Pubblico. These didn't only show secular figures, they featured landscapes too. However the Lorenzettis died in the Black Death, which decimated Siena's population. Important artists, such as Domenico Beccafumi and Il Sodoma (p73) followed, but the Golden Age of Sienese painting was essentially over.

★ **Views**

Best

- Torre del Mangia, p36 and p197
- Panorama at the Museo dell'Opera del Duomo, p45
- Top of the Centro Arte Contemporanea, p51
- Torre Grossa, San Gimignano, p79
- The balcony at Key Largo, p125

ground, covered by glass, are the remains of an 8th-century food store, while the walls are dotted with medieval graffiti. You can also see the arch that supports the pulpit in the cathedral above.

Battistero di San Giovanni

Piazza San Giovanni, **T** 0577 283048. *Mid Mar-end Sept 0900-1930, Oct 0900-1800, Nov-mid Mar 1000-1300, 1400-1700.* €3. *Map 2, B3, p236*

The gorgeous Baptistry, also called San Giovanni, was built between 1316 and 1325 by Camaino di Crescentino, father of Tino di Camaino. It is underneath the choir of the Duomo and is reached by a long set of marble stairs – look for the one marked with a cross; it's where St Catherine is said to have fallen and broken her tooth. Every inch seems to be covered with jewel-bright frescoes, painted in the 15th century by Lorenzo di Pietro (Il Vecchietta) and Michele di Matteo. The star is the **baptismal font** to which all the major Italian Renaissance sculptors contributed. Commissioned in 1416, it took 20 years to complete. It's decorated with gilded bronze panels depicting the life of the Baptist, and includes Ghiberti's *Baptism of Christ*, Jacopo della Quercia's *Annunciation of the Baptist to Zacharias* and an extremely vivid *Herod's Feast* by Donatello.

★ Spedale di Santa Maria della Scala

Piazza del Duomo, **T** 0577 224811, www.santamaria.siena.it. *Summer 1030-1830, winter 1030-1630 . €6 (€5.50 if booked in advance). Map 2, D1, p236*

Stretched in front of the Duomo, this was once the city's hospital, one of the first in Europe, and was still treating patients in the 1980s. Now it's being turned into a museum complex, with unmissable examples of secular art.

Legend dates it to the 9th century when a cobbler named Sorore opened a hostel for travellers. In fact, it was set up by canons from the cathedral to provide hospitality and medical care for pilgrims. It also took in abandoned children, *gettatelli*. Donations to it have been recorded as early as 1090 and by the 14th century it came under control of the city rather than the church. The building incorporates the church of **Santissima Annunziata** (*left at entrance, free*) which dates back to the 13th century. Above the altar there's a painting of a miraculous healing, *Probatica Piscina* (1730), by Sebastiano Conca. There's also a signed bronze of the *Risen Christ* by Il Vecchietta.

The labyrinthine hospital complex was further developed in the 14th and 15th centuries. The most important room is undoubtedly the **Sala del Pellegrinaio**, an extremely unlikely ward that was still in use until the 1980s. An airy blue expanse, its walls are smothered with frescoes that lovingly record the daily life and legends of the hospital. Painted between 1440 and 1444 by Il Vecchietta, Domenico di Bartolo and other artists, they were the brainchild of Rector Giovanni di Francesco Buzzichelli and their secular content makes them unique: food is given to the poor; a bishop distributes alms; and the sick are tended. Most famous is *Il Governo e la Cura degli Infermi*, in which a patient is helped onto a stretcher while doctors carefully examine a specimen of urine.

Surrounding rooms are being restored at the time of writing, but downstairs you can see an exhibition on the restoration of the Fonte Gaia, the original fountain from Il Campo. Turn right at the bottom of the stairs and there's a gloomy corridor leading to the **Oratorio di Santa Caterina della Notte**, a grim, oppressive and extremely creepy chapel where St Catherine used to come to pray. Continue downstairs and you come to a 12th-century chamber once used by the lay council of the hospital. Right down in the bowels of the hospital is the **Museo Archeologico**, where shadowy tunnels cut into the tufa are filled with artefacts and finds from excavations around Siena, including some from tombs of the 6th century BC.

Pinacoteca Nazionale

Via San Pietro, **T** 0577 281161. *Mon 0830-1330, Wed-Sat 0830-1915, Sun 0815-1315. €4. Map 2, E4, p236*

The city's art gallery is devoted to Sienese art from the 13th century, with a dazzling array of paintings embellished with gold leaf – a legacy of the Sienese school's adherence to the Byzantine tradition. Comprehensive though it is, it's less likely to absorb the casual visitor than the specialist, so if you feel you've seen enough religious painting, don't feel guilty about giving it a miss. Among the most important works is the tiny *Madonna dei Francescani*, by Duccio, probably painted in 1285, pre-dating his *Maestà* for the Duomo. Other works include Simone Martini's *Madonna and Child*, Pietro Lorenzetti's *Madonna Enthroned*, *The Adoration of the Magi* by Taddeo di Bartolo and works by Il Sodoma (p73), Beccafumi and Guido da Siena. Look out for two charming and extremely detailed landscapes, *A City on the Sea* and *A Castle on the Shore*. Said to be the first examples of pure landscape painting, they were originally thought to be the work of Ambrogio Lorenzetti, but have now been attributed to Sassetta. The gallery also contains cartoons by Beccafumi, some of which were used to create panels in the floor of the Duomo.

Palazzo Chigi Saracini

Via di Città 89, **T** 0577 22091. *Library Mon-Fri 0930-1230, Jul and Aug 1000-1300, 1530-1700; Musical Instrument Museum, phone first to arrange appointment; Palace 0900-1930 until Jun 2005; after that, telephone to arrange appointment. Map 2, C4, p236*

This palace dates back to the 12th century, but was remodelled in later years by a succession of Siena's most powerful families. It's now the seat of the prestigious Fondazione Accademia Musicale Chigiana, founded by Count Guido Chigi Saracini. The **library** contains a shelf-breaking 70,000 volumes including rare sheet music. The **Musical Instrument Museum** fills three rooms, and contains everything from violins to mandolins and rare harpsichords made by craftsmen like Stradivarius and Amati. The **palace** itself has a stunning art collection, with paintings from the 13th to 19th centuries as well as ceramics, porcelain and silver.

Palazzo delle Papesse

126 Via di Città, **T** 0577 22071. *Tue-Sun 1200-1900 (approx). €5. Map 2, D4, p236*

Designed by Rossellino and built for Pope Pius II's sister Caterina Piccolomini in the 15th century, the palace was altered in the 19th century when it was acquired by the Bank of Italy. Now it houses the **Centro Arte Contemporanea**, with the bank's former strongroom hosting various exhibits. There are no permanent displays so you might find anything from conceptual art to films, done by a range of international artists. Bring your camera: at the very top, there's a terrace with eye-stretching panoramic views of the city and surrounding hills.

Chiesa di Sant'Agostino

Prato di Sant'Agostino. *1100-1300, 1400-1730. €2. Map 2, D4, p236*

By the square where the Contrada della Tartuca (Turtle) hold their celebratory dinners, this Gothic church was nearly burnt to the ground in the 18th century and was rebuilt by Luigi Vanvitelli. The church is no longer used for services, just occasional concerts. It justifies its entrance fee with a flamboyant marble altar, frescoes by Ambrogio Lorenzetti in the **Piccolomini** chapel and a lovely *Epiphany* by Il Sodoma (p73). Most unusual are the recently restored monochrome frescoes in the **Bichi** family chapel. They've been attributed to Sienese artist Francesco di Giorgio Martini (1439-1501/2). There is also work by Luca Signorelli, and the floor is covered with painted majolica tiles.

Orto Botanico

Via Pier Andrea Mattioli 4, *T 0577 235415. Mon-Fri 0800-1230, 1430-1730, Sat 0800-1200. Free. Map 2, H3, p236 See also p197*

Part of the university, this botanical garden provides a rare cool, green haven within the city walls. It is laid out in terraces, dotted with seats, and contains Tuscan plants, orchids, mosses and trees such as Ginkgo biloba, fig, peach and persimmon. Walk down to the bottom and you'll reach a tranquil patch of grass by an old stone pool and a section of old city wall – a good spot for picnic.

Museo di Storia Naturale

Via Pier Andrea Mattioli. *Sun-Wed and Fri 0900-1300, 1500-1800, Thu 0900-1300, closed Sat. Free. Map 2, G4, p236. See also p197*

There's a somewhat dusty feel to this traditional collection of fossils, rocks, stuffed animals and skeletons, owned by the university. The large beaked skelton of a fin whale in the courtyard might satisfy younger kids on a wet day.

Cimitero Monumentale della Misericordia

Follow Via Pier Andrea Mattioli through the Porta Tufi.
Map 2, H5, p236 (off map)

Cemeteries aren't top of every visitor's hit list, but this one, outside the city walls, contains some of Siena's most important 19th-century artworks. There are chapels belonging to the wealthiest families, a marble *Pietà* by Giovanni Duprè, and sculptures and frescoes by Tito Sarrocchi, Cesare Maccari and many others.

Terzo di Camollia

Taking its name from the Porta Camollia, this area covers the northern part of the city and its furthest reaches attract fewest tourists. It faces Florence, the enemy to the north, and, as it was always vulnerable to attack, became the most fortified part of the city. Via di Camollia and Via Banchi di Sopra were part of the ancient religious roadway, the Via Francigena, and for hundreds of years pilgrims tramped along here on their way to Rome. Today Via Banchi di Sopra is lined with Siena's smartest shops and coolest cafés. It's also the focus of the evening passeggiata, the nightly stroll that attracts a chic throng of locals: cool, snappily dressed and wearing sunglasses whatever the weather. The terrain has led to this being the most developed part of the city and squeezed beside the glowering fortress are more prosaic 20th-century developments, like the bus station, post office and football stadium. Yet due to the Via Francigena this terzo also has a large number of 13th- and 14th-century buildings, many of which were former pilgrims' hostels. Pilgrims still come here: St Catherine of Siena was born in this district and her former home attracts large numbers of devout visitors.

▸▸ *See Sleeping p105, Eating and drinking p132, Bars and clubs p156*

! The Orto Botanico is reputed to be haunted by the ghost of Giacomo del Sodoma 'Giomo', a monk and painter who is said to wander around making noises and throwing things at people.

Basilica di San Domenico

Piazza San Domenico. *Summer 0900-1830, Nov-Easter 0830-1800. Free. Map 3, F5, p238*

Perched on a steep escarpment above the Fontebranda valley, this enormous brick church (13th century) was built by the Dominicans. There was once an ambitious plan to bridge the valley, linking it to the cathedral on the other side but it never went ahead. It's vast and empty inside, and its most important works of art focus on St Catherine, who was said to have performed some of her miracles here. The **Cappella di Santa Caterina** is covered with frescoes of her life by Il Sodoma (p73), the artist who introduced the Leonardo style of painting to Siena. Rather alarmingly it also contains a holy relic: her preserved head in a glass case. Her famous broken tooth – she fell on the steps by the Baptistry – is clearly visible. Other cases contain one of her fingers and the whip with which she beat herself. To the right-hand side of the door is Andrea Vanni's *Portrait of St Catherine*; the only work completed in her lifetime, it's thought to be a realistic likeness.

Fortezza Medicea

Enoteca Toscana, **T** 0577 226989. *1000-2000. Map 3, C2, p238*

The conquering Florentines set their stamp on Siena by building this sturdy fortress, made from one million bricks. Its brick arches now house a state *enoteca*, promoting Italy's finest wines. There's a huge selection (over 1,000) of different wines for sale. A few are available for tasting, starting at €2 per glass, and there's a little patio. They'll ship bottles anywhere you want. If you don't want wine you can simply go for a walk round the ramparts.

▶ Siena's ascetic saint

The Sienese have enormous respect for their patron saint, Catherine of Siena (1347-1380), not to be confused with the Roman martyr who's remembered with Catherine Wheels. She was one of 25 children and, from a very young age, showed signs of being distinctly different from other children. She began having visions when she was very young and at around seven declared she would remain a virgin. When her family tried to marry her off in her teens, she flatly refused – cutting off her hair in protest. Against her parents' will she entered the Dominican order and for three years lived like a hermit in her own home. Her life was ascetic in the extreme: she regularly flagellated herself, had a stone for a pillow and apparently survived for years eating only communion wafers. Her visions continued, including one in which she married Christ, and she eventually rejoined the world and began to care for the needy. When she received the stigmata in 1375, her fame spread. She became increasingly political and corresponded with the most powerful people in Europe – dictating her letters since she was illiterate. In 1378 she went to Avignon and convinced the pope to move the papal court from France back to Rome. She died in Rome aged 33 and was later canonized by the Sienese Pope, Pius II. She's now Patron Saint of Italy (together with St Francis), Patron Saint of Europe and, an unusual honour for a woman, a Doctor of the church.

Santuario e Casa di Santa Caterina

Costa di Sant'Antonio, *T* 0577 247 393. *0915-1230, 1500-1900. Free. Map 3, F7, p239*

St Catherine's home was turned into a sanctuary in the 15th century. On one side is the **Oratorio del Crocifisso**, built in

> ### The Battle of Montaperti

Florence was traditionally Siena's enemy: fiercely independent states, they not only rubbed borders, there was constant competition between their bankers and merchants. In addition, medieval Italian cities and families were torn by conflict between the **Guelphs**, the supporters of the Pope, and the pro-imperial **Ghibellines** who supported the Emperor, Frederick the Great. Allegiances of the cities changed, but Siena and Florence always made sure they were on opposing sides. Envious of Siena's increasing wealth, the Florentines (then Guelphs) tried to block the city's trade routes, building fortresses at strategic points. In 1260 their army, on its way to fortify their base at Montalcino, stopped near Siena at Montaperti. They sent ambassadors to the city demanding surrender. The Sienese prayed for assistance from the Madonna and then, supported by exiled Florentine Ghibellines, attacked the enemy camp and won a decisive vistory. It's still remembered in the city – even though Florence eventually conquered Siena anyway.

rococo style to house the Pisan painting in front of which St Catherine was said to have received the stigmata. Opposite is the family's old kitchen, now an oratory; the fireplace is under the altar. The floor is covered with blue and yellow majolica tiles. Downstairs is St Catherine's cell, now covered with 19th-century frescoes of important episodes in her life – including her cutting off her long hair. Another painting of her, with Mary, shows the switch with which she regularly beat herself. The tiny bedroom contains holy relics.

● *A short walk from here is the* **Fonte Branda**, *one of the largest fountains in the city. It dates back to at least 1081 and was enlarged in later years. It looks a bit like a mini fortress and contained four basins, for drinking water, for animals, for washing and for industry. It was mentioned by Dante in his* Divine Comedy.

Via Banchi di Sopra
Map 3, G10, p239

Once part of the Via Francigena, this is now the city's smartest street with shops like Max Mara and the famous Nannini café/bar. This is where the evening *passeggiata* takes place – the see-and-be-seen stroll that takes place in all Italian cities. Many fine old buildings and palaces line the street and reminders of the glory days are everywhere – not many branches of Benetton have 16th-century frescoes on the ceiling. The oldest Gothic palace is the **Palazzo Tolomei**, which dominates Piazza Tolomei. It was once the seat of one of the city's most powerful families of merchants and bankers. At the junction with Banchi di Sotto there's the **Loggia della Mercanzia**, the court of the city's merchants, where the daily rate of exchange was set. It was here that pilgrims had to choose whether to continue along Banchi di Sotto to Rome, or turn down Via di Città to Siena's cathedral. The faces of the statues on the columns all look north, up Banchi di Sopra, inviting pilgrims to break their journey in Siena. This point also roughly marks the meeting of the *terzi*, the city's three districts.

Palazzo Salimbeni
Piazza Salimbeni, **T** 0577 294111. *Visits by appointment only.*
Map 3, D9, p239

Palazzo Salimbeni is the headquarters of the **Monte dei Paschi** bank, founded in 1472 and probably the oldest in the world. The bank grew from the practice of charging shepherds to graze their sheep on the pastures (*paschi*) in the Maremma region. The money was then used

! The first Italian bankers worked from a bench (*banco*) in the street. If the city decided to stop them trading the bench was broken (*rotto*); hence the Italian for bankrupt, *bancarotta*.

► Via Francigena

The Via Francigena was first documented in the year 990 by Sigeric, then Archbishop of Canterbury, who was obliged to travel to Rome to receive the *pallium* (a symbolic woollen stole) from the Pope. The record, listing the places at which he stopped, is now preserved in the British Library. The road evolved over the years and alternative routes were established, creating in the end a trans-European highway for pilgrims and merchants. It could be an arduous and dangerous journey, and once travellers reached the north of Italy, they risked malarial swamps to the west, and robbers and bandits in the mountains to the east.

The safest route was through Siena. Hospitals, offering both hospitality and healthcare, sprang up along the way – like the Spedale di Santa Maria della Scala. By the Middle Ages pilgrimages had become big business, almost medieval package tours: itineraries featured churches and holy relics instead of today's art treasures and Armani. With no rivers, Siena could neither work materials nor easily transport goods, so the Via Francigena provided an economic lifeline. The city grew wealthy providing hospitality and banking facilities – something that made it very attractive to its rival city-state, Florence.

to make loans. The Via Francigena brought thousands of foreign visitors, increasing the banking trade still more. Many moneylenders charged very high interest, but the Monte dei Paschi bank charged less. It has a long tradition of commissioning and purchasing works of art and now has a fine collection. The bank sponsors cultural events in the city and often contributes to building restoration. Most Sienese still bank here.

Basilica di San Francesco

Piazza San Francesco. *End of Via dei Rossi. 0730-1200, 1530-1900. Free. Map 3, C12, p239*

You don't appreciate the scale of this church until you're inside: it's like a huge empty barn, the darkness only relieved by zebra stripes of marble. Built in the late 14th century, it was later badly damaged by fire. Inside are works by the Lorenzetti brothers. The adjoining cloisters are part of the university – the crypt is now the library.

Oratorio di San Bernardino and Museo Diocesano d'Arte Sacra

Piazza San Francesco, **T** 0577 283048, www.operaduomo.siena.it. *Mar-Oct 1030-1330, 1500-1730. €3. Map 3, D12, p239*

This oratory marks the spot where St Bernardino prayed and preached while in Siena. There are two chapels here. The lower one was frescoed by leading 17th-century Sienese painters. The upper chapel is an example of High Renaissance art, the walls covered with frescoes illustrating stories of the Virgin, by Beccafumi, Il Sodoma (p73) and Girolamo del Pacchia (1477-c1533). The museum contains important works such as the *Madonna del Latte* (a breast-feeding Madonna), by Ambrogio Lorenzetti, and the Byzantine-style work by Maestro di Tressa of an early 13th-century Madonna with particularly large eyes.

Listings

● Museums and galleries

- **Museo Civico** Inside the magnificent Palazzo Pubblico, it contains Siena's oldest fresco and Simone Martini's fine *Maestà*, p32.
- **Museo delle Tavolette di Biccherna** Siena's unsung treasure in a 14th-century palace: extraordinary painted book covers depicting ancient city life, p37.
- **Museo dell'Opera del Duomo** Many treasures from the cathedral including the painting that founded the Sienese school, p45.
- **Spedale di Santa Maria della Scala** One of the world's oldest hospitals, now a museum with fine frescoed walls, p49.
- **Museo Archeologico** Finds from excavations around Siena, including some from 6th century BC, p50.
- **Pinacoteca Nazionale** The city's art gallery crammed with gilded pictures of the Sienese school of painting, p50.
- **Musical Instrument Museum** (Palazzo Chigi Saracini) Richly decorated palace that contains a museum filled with rare musical instruments, p51.
- **Centro Arte Contemporanea** Changing exhibitions of international contemporary art in a 15th-century palace, p51.
- **Orto Botanico** The university's botanical garden filled with Tuscan plants and cool mosses and ferns, p52.
- **Museo di Storia Naturale** Stuffed animals and ancient rocks at this university natural history museum, p52.
- **Museo Diocesano d'Arte Sacra** Charming, small museum containing some important gilded Madonnas, p59.
- **Museo d'Arte per Bambini** Lots of activities at this museum that aims to make art fun for kids. p197.

South of Siena 63 Picture-postcard Tuscany with rolling hills, fields of sunflowers and famous wines. Immaculately preserved hilltop towns such as Pienza, and ancient abbeys like glorious Monte Oliveto Maggiore.

West of Siena 75 San Gimignano, the medieval city with famous, lofty grey towers; Monteriggioni, an isolated fortification; Colle di Val d'Elsa, a hill town that's the home of fine crystal, and Volterra, the ancient base of the mysterious Etruscans.

North of Siena 87 Chianti, the famous wine region stretching north from Siena to Florence; vineyards, sleepy country roads, little villages, craggy hills and dense oakwoods; ideal for exploring by car or on a bike.

East of Siena 90 The Piero della Francesca trail: lively Arezzo, famous for his fabulous fresco cycle; Sansepolcro, his birthplace and home to 'the greatest painting in the world'; and the tiny village of Monterchi, where a miraculous Madonna is unveiled. Also the picturesque hill town of Cortona, with lots of bars and restaurants, eye-stretching views and an Etruscan chandelier.

South of Siena

This is quintessential Tuscany – a rolling landscape dotted with immaculately preserved hill towns and ancient abbeys, punctuated with cypress trees that pierce the sky like dark green daggers. The area was once ravaged by power struggles between the Sienese and the Florentines; now it's tranquil. The pace of life is slow, and most people work with olives, wine or tourism – sometimes all three. The fabric of life seems remarkably unruffled by the 21st century and people still feel great allegiance to their village or hamlet. The best-known places, like Montalcino, get busy in high summer so it's better to come in spring or autumn. There are two distinct landscapes: the **Val d'Orcia**, which is soft and picturesque, fertile and rather dreamy; and the **Crete Senese** which is starker with smooth waves of clay soil rippled by *calanchi* – rivers of erosion, long curvy roads and cheery fields of sunflowers. Much of the area is now a UNESCO site and it's the sort of place that has you pulling out your camera every few minutes. Film-makers visit frequently: *The English Patient* was shot here, as were *A Midsummer Night's Dream* and *Gladiator*. Most visitors come for the fine red wines, the star being Brunello from Montalcino.

▶▶ *See Sleeping p110, Eating and drinking p135, Bars and clubs p158*

You can reach some of the towns by bus from Siena, but you often have to change and will certainly miss a great deal; it's far easier to explore by car.

San Quirico d'Orcia and around

Don't be put off by the dull modern outskirts, the centre of the village is charming. Its origins are Etruscan but its heyday was in medieval times; 40 km from Siena, it was an important stopping place on the busy Via Francigena and it has a number of atmospheric medieval churches.

▶ **Drives in southern Tuscany**

There are so many towns and villages worth seeing that you could easily spend several days exploring. One route might be to take the SR2 from Siena to **Buonconvento**, a low-lying town with a medieval heart and the little Museo d'Arte Sacra (T 0577 807181, *Tue-Sun in summer, weekends in winter*, €3) containing medieval painting and religious treasures. From there you can make for **San Giovanni d'Asso** and nearby **Monte Oliveto Maggiore**. Minor roads will then snake through the countryside to **Torrita di Siena** where you bear south for **Montepulciano**, then follow the SS146 to **Pienza**. From here you can continue to **San Quirico d'Orcia** where the SS2 leads back to Buonconvento.

For a longer drive head south to see the Roman pool at **Bagno Vignoni**. Minor roads lead from here to **Castiglione d'Orcia**, then on to **Monte Amiata**, and past **Abbazia di Sant' Antimo** to Montalcino. Go north on the SP45 to **Buonconvento** and back to Siena. The key is not to rush things and pack everything into one day, otherwise all the sights will merge into one.

 Sights

La Collegiata
Piazza Chigi, off Via Corso. *Daily. Free.*

The 12th-century Romanesque Collegiata, the greatest attraction in the village, was built on the site of an 8th-century parish church and has three impressive entrances, with Lombard-influenced carvings: all of them faced the Via Francigena – encouraging pilgrims to stop and take a look. There's a slightly incongruous rococo altarpiece and inlaid wooden choir stalls behind the altar originally made by Antonio Barili for Siena's

Cortona
*ears were said to pour down Fra Angelico's face as he
ainted his Annunciation in Cortona's Museo Diocesano.*

1 *Siena's Torre del Mangia gets its name from one of the first bellringers, a lazy, fat man nicknamed* Mangia-guadagni *– 'eat the profits'.* ▶▶ *See page 36.*

2 *In August the hilltop town of Montepulciano, best known for its fine* vino nobile, *hosts the historic Bruscello festival and the barrel-rolling Bravio delle Botti.* ▶▶ *See pages 72 and 173.*

3 *Winemaking in Tuscany goes back thousands of years to Etruscan times. The S222, known as the* chiantigiana, *makes a good wine route.* ▶▶ *See pages 88 and 220.*

4 *Delicatessen heaven; stock up on fresh olive oil, cold meats, pungent* pecorino *cheese, almondy* ricciarelli *and rich slabs of* panforte, *then head off for a picnic.* ▶▶ *See page 181.*

5 *Quintessential Tuscany: a rolling landscape punctuated with cypress trees that pierce the sky like dark green daggers.* ▶▶ *See page 63.*

6 *Pretty Cortona, besieged by tourists ever since the publication of* Under the Tuscan Sun, *is still a good base for exploring the villages of the Valdichiana.* ▶▶ *See page 97.*

Fonte Gaia
The fountain in the Piazza del Campo is a 19th-century copy of the original, which is displayed in the Spedale di Santa Maria della Scala.

Flag waving
The medieval tradition of flag waving forms part of the pageantry of Siena's famous Palio.

Sunshine and flowers
Beyond Siena, seductive Tuscany lives up to its stereotype: vineyards, hilltop towns, cypress trees and fields of cheery sunflowers.

Palazzo Pubblico
The 13th-century Palazzo Pubblico was built to impress; a symbol of the city's independence and power.

Il Campo from the Torre del Mangia
In honour of its creators, the Council of Nine (p211), the medieval piazza is divided into nine equal segments.

Il Palio
If the jockeys fall off during Siena's world-famous race it doesn't matter; the horse that finishes first is the winner, riderless or not.

San Biagio
Just outside Montepulciano, this is one of the most important churches of the Renaissance.

Duomo. Unfortunately it's hard to see them. To one side of the altar there's a gilded triptych by Sano di Pietro, a Sienese painter, pupil and follower of Sassetta – put 50 cents in the box to illuminate it.

● *Near the church is the* **Chigi Palace**, *which was badly damaged in the Second World War and is now gradually being restored.*

Chiesa Santa Maria
Via Dante Alighieri. *Daily. Free.*

Also known as Santa Maria ad Hortos because it was once surrounded by orchards, this small Romanesque church dates back to the 11th century. There are two entrances: one very simple, the other – which faced the Via Francigena – ornate. On the opposite side of the road is a former hospital where pilgrims could shelter.

● *Another church, the* **Chiesa della Madonna di Vitaleta** *on the main square, has a sculpture of the Madonna on the high altar by Andrea della Robbia. Just off the main square is a Renaissance garden,* **Horti Leonini** *(Porta Nuovo, entry free) which was created in 1580 and has formal box hedges and statues.*

Villa Malintoppo
Strada delle Foramcci, **T** 0577 897524. *Daily. Just outside San Quirico d'Orcia.*

This elegant villa, owned by the Simonelli-Santi family, is a good place to come to try the local *Orcia* DOC wines and organic olive oil. Tastings and guided tours are on offer.

! On the SS2, 4 km from San Quirico d'Orcia and just by a bridge, is a small group of cypress trees breaking the smooth landscape; they're the ones that feature on all the postcards.

Bagno Vignoni
4 km southeast of San Quirico d'Orcia on the SS2. See also p198

The great and the good once came here; not to pray, but to bathe in the steaming waters of the pool that forms this hamlet's main square. The hot springs were known to the Etruscans, but it took those professional bathers the Romans to transform the area into a spa. In medieval times travellers following the Via Francigena stopped here to treat their aching limbs in the sulphurous water. St Catherine of Siena and Pope Pius II both took the waters, and Lorenzo de' Medici was so keen he built the Renaissance loggia. You can't bathe in the central pool – the water reaches 52Cº – but there are a couple of hotels: the **Posta Marucci** (T 0577 887112, www.hotelpostamarucci.it), allows non-residents day passes to use their spa (*Fri-Wed 0900-1300, 1430-1800, Thu 0900-1300; €10, €7 on Thu; massages €50*), while **Le Terme** (T 0577 887365) has facilities for residents only.

★ Abbazia di Monte Oliveto Maggiore
Asciano, T 0577 707611. 0915-1200, 1530-1730. Free. From Siena you can take the 438 to Asciano and then 451 to the abbey, or go to Buonconvento and then pick up the road.

A fragrant tree-lined path leads to this gloriously isolated Benedictine abbey, founded in 1313 by Sienese nobleman Bernardo Tolomei. A hermitage of Olivetans, or White Benedictines, grew up. They lived extremely simply at first, but eventually the order grew incredibly wealthy and the charm of humble living faded somewhat. In the **church** there are intricate inlaid choir stalls by Giovanni da Verona in 1505. They depict birds, musical instruments and views – the first to be done in wood. Mass is still sung daily in Gregorian chant (*Mon-Fri 0800 and 1815, Sun 0845, 1100 and 1830*).

The main draw is the **cloisters**, their walls smothered with 15th-century frescoes of the life of St Benedict. The first eight, showing scenes from his later life, were by Luca Signorelli; the remainder by Il Sodoma. The combination of landscapes, lively narrative and attention to detail make them compelling. One, in which St Benedict helps a cripple, includes a self portrait of Il Sodoma (p71) – together with his pet badgers. Others show a monk being scourged, St Benedict supervising building projects, and a group of prostitutes cheerily tempting the monks. You can go upstairs to the old library and an ancient pharmacy full of decorative storage vases. Get here early to try and beat the tour buses. It gets incredibly busy.

San Giovanni d'Asso

Museo del Tartufo, beside the castello, **T** 0577 803101.
Hours vary, weekends 1000-1300, 1400-1800. €3. See also p199

San Giovanni's famed for its truffles, particularly the white variety (the type that a London restaurant recently bought for thousands of pounds, then left in the fridge to rot while the head chef went on holiday). This new museum covers the history and folklore of the famed fungus – once considered the food of witches. There's a film on truffle hunting, traditionally done with dogs, as well as some scratch and sniff displays.

Montalcino

Wine lovers all over the world have heard of Montalcino, home of the famous – and famously expensive – Brunello di Montalcino. It's aged for four or more years before going on sale. The town sits perkily on a hilltop, surrounded by vineyards and glorious countryside. It was the last of the towns in the Sienese Republic to surrender to Florence.

Sights

La Fortezza
Piazzale Fortezza, **T** 0577 849211. *Apr-Oct daily 0900-2000, Nov-Mar Mon-Sat 0900-1800.*

The town's dominant feature, this 14th-century fortress, is a reminder of Montalcino's strategic position on the Via Francigena. It was Siena's greatest ally. Now it's been turned into a pleasant *enoteca*, with a wide choice of wines and olive oils to taste and buy. They've got 130 different types of Brunello alone. It's well worth walking up onto the **old ramparts** (€3.50); there are head-spinning views of the Val d'Orcia.

Museo Civico e Diocesano
Via Ricasoli 31, **T** 0577 846014. *Tue-Sun 1000-1300, 1400-1740. €4.50 (€6 combined ticket with La Fortezza).*

Art from the 13th to 16th centuries is featured here, including pieces by Bartolo di Fredi, who worked on many of Montalcino's churches in the 14th century. Other artists respresented are Il Vecchietta and Simone Martini, and there are valuable painted wooden sculptures, early majolica mugs and some illuminated texts.

Abbazia di Sant'Antimo
Castelnuovo dell'Abate, **T** 0577 835659. *Mon-Sat 1030-1230, 1500-1830, Sun 0900-1030, 1500-1800. Free. 10 km from Montalcino.*

! If your budget doesn't quite stretch to *Brunello*, try some of the other local wines which are excellent and a lot cheaper. *Rosso di Montalcino* is a good bet. The countryside is covered with wineries you can visit – ask the tourist office for details.

Set in lush green countryside, this soft, honey-stone abbey was reputedly founded by Charlemagne (AD 781) as thanks for saving his troops from disease. The present Romanesque church was built in the early 12th century in French style – evident in the ambulatory, a walkway round the altar with radiating chapels – and the design is unique in Tuscany. Inside is a wooden Crucifix (12th century), and a carving of *Daniel in the Lion's Den* on the capital of one of the columns. Mass is still sung in Gregorian chant (times are available from the tourist office in Montalcino).

● *There's an enjoyably easy walk from Sant'Antimo along an old Roman road. A brown sign in the abbey car park indicates the start, with red and white flashes on trees along the way. Walk to a stone hut, then fork left through quiet woods and olive groves. Go right at the next fork and you'll eventually climb uphill to La Magia farmhouse. Turn right and walk into **Villa a Tolli**, a lovely sleepy hamlet with several wineries. Friendly locals will often show you around. From here you can continue to Montalcino or walk back to the abbey.*

Pienza

A visit here is a trip to Utopia – at least one man's idea of it. Originally known as Corsignano, the tiny medieval village was transformed in 1459 by Pope Pius II (p71), who had decided to turn his birthplace into an ideal Renaissance city. The work was carried out by the Florentine architect Bernardo Rossellino, who cleverly redeveloped the centre without destroying the medieval layout. It was later renamed Pienza. Both the Pope and his architect died before work could be completed, but it's still the most memorable of places. Italians often come out for Sunday lunch and a stroll around the walls. Take Via dell'Amore (love) or Via del Bacio (kiss) to reach the city walls. There are spectacular views to Monte Amiata.

Sights

Duomo

Piazza Pio II. *Daily. Free.*

The crack in the wall of the cathedral clearly illustrates the fact that it's gradually slipping downhill. It started sinking shortly after it was built and despite attempts to halt it, still moves a bit every year. It's light and bright inside, as the Pope wanted it to be a *domus vitrea* (house of glass) to symbolize intellectual enlightenment. He commissioned paintings by skilled Sienese artists which still hang here today, including a masterly *Assumption* by Il Vecchietta.

Museo Diocesano

Corso Rosellino 30, **T** 0578 749905. *Wed-Mon 1000-1300, 1500-1800, closed Tue. €4.*

This museum houses a wonderfully eclectic mix of medieval paintings, sculptures and other treasures. Look out for a *Madonna and Child* by Pietro Lorenzetti and the cope, embroidered in England, that belonged to Pope Pius II.

● *Via delle Case Nuove, near the church of San Carlo, contains small, neat houses that were built specifically for the working people. It was part of Pius' humanist vision – a small forerunner to ideal English industrial towns such as New Lanark and Bournville.*

!
● Pienza's renowned for its pungent *pecorino* cheese, a sheep's cheese that's often drizzled with honey. It can be eaten fresh, when it's soft and white, or aged, when it's hard and cream coloured, the rind often seasoned with tomato or even ashes. You can buy it everywhere.

▶ The people's pope

If ever there was a Renaissance man it was Pope Pius II (1405-1464), often known as the first humanist. Enea Silvius de' Piccolomini was born in the Val d'Orcia to a wealthy family. He studied in Siena, then embarked on a successful diplomatic career. He first moved to Switzerland, then to Scotland, where he was ambassador to James II. Later he became secretary to Emperor Frederick III, who made him poet laureate. He was a free thinker; loved nature and the arts, and was a prolific author, writing books and poetry – including an autobiographical diary. He also loved women and fathered at least two illegitimate children. At 40 he dramatically changed his life and became a priest. He was no less successful at that and was soon made a cardinal – by the age of 53 he was Pope. After Constantinople fell to the Ottoman Turks he called for Europe to embark on a crusade to free it – but it never got further than Ancona where Pius, by then an old man, fell ill and died.

Palazzo Piccolomini
Piazza Pio II, 2. *Tue-Sun 1000-1230, 1500-1800, closed Mon. €3, guided tours only.*

Commissioned by Pius, this fine residence was home to members of his family until 1962. The tour takes you round the state apartments, including his bedroom and library. There's also an ornate courtyard and gorgeous hanging gardens with views right across the Sienese valleys.

● *Not far from Pienza is* **Sant'Anna in Camprena**, *a monastery that was founded in 1324-1334 and rebuilt in Renaissance times. The refectory is decorated with frescoes by Giovanni Antonio Bazzi, known as* Il Sodoma (p73), *and were his first major commission. They featured in the film* The English Patient. *Ask Pienza APT for information.*

Montepulciano

This hill town, about 43 km south of Siena, dominates the flat Valdichiana, a once marshy area where high ground was of both strategic and economic importance. Wealthy Florentines would come to spend the summer here and there are plenty of Renaissance buildings to admire. Wine's the big attraction though: the town's most famous product is Vino Nobile di Montepulciano.

Sights

Duomo
Piazza Grande. *Daily. Free.*

The Duomo's façade is unfinished, but inside you'll find an eye-catching altarpiece, created in 1401 by Taddeo di Bartolo. It's painted on wood and lavished with real gold. There's also work by Andrea della Robbia (1435-1525) and fragments of Michelozzo's (1396-1472) tomb of Bartolomeo Aragazzi. The Duomo is the main sight on Piazza Grande, which, as its name suggests, is the main square. It's ringed by imposing palaces – such as the Palazzo Comunale and the Palazzo Tarugi – and contains the town's old well.

Museo Civico
Via Ricci 10, *T* 0578 717300. *Tue-Sun winter 1000-1300, 1500-1800, summer 1000-1300, 1500-1900. €4. North of the Piazza Grande.*

Situated in the ancient Palazzo Neri-Orselli, the town museum is essentially divided into an art gallery and archaeological museum. The gallery has a wide range of works by Tuscan painters from the 14th to 17th centuries. Among them is a

▶ Colourful character

Giovanni Antonio Bazzi (1477-1549) was one of Siena's more flamboyant characters. Born in Lombardy, he moved to Siena as a young artist, where he acquired his nickname 'Il Sodoma' – the sodomite. Some think it was a corruption of a family name: Sodona, but Giorgio Vasari, evidently not a fan, described him in a contemporary account as eccentric and self indulgent, surrounding himself with 'boys and beardless youths of whom he was inordinately fond'. The artist good humouredly adopted the name and used it to sign his work. He married and had children, but was noted for painting androgynous figures. He was influenced by Leonardo when young and was later invited to Rome to paint the bedroom of the Sienese banker Agostino Chigi. He was certainly individual, dressing gaudily, cracking jokes, composing bawdy poems – and keeping a menagerie of exotic pets that Vasari disapprovingly referred to as a 'Noah's ark'. When he got older he stopped bothering to make cartoons (preparatory drawings) for his frescoes. Most of his best work is in Siena, where he died in the hospital on St Valentine's Day.

painting of the *Holy Family* by Il Sodoma (p73), and a *Madonna and Child*, recently attributed to Duccio di Buoninsegna. There are also some terracotta statues by Andrea della Robbia. Among the ancient stonework and pottery pieces, you'll find a silver *Funeral Mask of St Agnes*.

● *Nearby Via di Gracciano nel Corso is the most important shopping street; make sure you stop to look at the covers of Etruscan tombs on the outside of Palazzo Bucelli.*

Buying wine

It's not difficult to find an *enoteca*; an amazing number claim to store the wine in genuine Etruscan tombs, but there are two particularly famous places to shop. **Azienda Agricola Contucci** (Palazzo Contucci, Via del Teatro, **T** 0578 757 006, www.contucci.it, *Mon-Fri 0830-1230, 1430-1830, longer in summer*) are the historic wine cellars of the aristocratic Contucci family who produce *Vino Nobile*; *Rosso di Monte-pulciano* and Sansovino, among others. You can visit the cellars, taste the wine and have bottles shipped home – and perhaps meet Adamo the friendly and helpful wine master who kisses all the ladies' hands, too. Past visitors have included Prince Charles and Tony Blair. Not far away is **Cantina del Redi** (Via Ricci, **T** 0578 756022, *1030-1300, 1500-1900*), the best-known and most photographed wine cellars in Montepulciano. They're reached by a long set of steps and are full of atmosphere, though the wine tends to be on the pricey side.

San Biagio
Via di San Biagio. *Daily. Free.*

If you're going to visit one church in town make it this one. About 15 minutes' walk from the centre it's the masterpiece of Antonio da Sangallo the Elder and was inaugurated in 1529. Sangallo was influenced by Bramante's designs for the reconstruction of St Peter's in Rome – although they never went ahead as planned. It's designed in the form of a Greek cross and is one of the most important churches of the Renaissance.

! Stand on the white circle in the centre of the church of San Biagio and check out the perfect echo. It only works from this spot.

West of Siena

The Sienese tend to sniff dismissively when you mention Volterra – it's part of the province of Pisa and therefore worthy of little interest. And the tourist's favourite, San Gimignano, is generally summed up with the words 'Ah, ruined!' followed by a sigh of regret. But don't be put off. San Gimignano's undeniably touristy but, with its fierce halo of towers, it is still an extraordinary sight. And the countryside round here and in the Val d'Elsa is classically Tuscan: silvery olive groves, cypresses, fields of sunflowers and numerous vineyards. Volterra, once described as 'a city of wind and rock', is filled with evidence of its Etruscan origins and is a good base for exploring a rougher, wilder landscape: thick oak woodlands, craggy hills and a geo-thermal area with thermal springs much like a witch's cauldron. The area's rich in wildlife and has plenty of tracks that offer interesting walking.

▶▶ *See Sleeping p113, Eating and drinking p139, Bars and clubs p158*

Buses run frequently from Siena to Colle di Val d'Elsa and the journey only takes about 30 mins. They run less frequently to San Gimignano and you might have to change in Colle. However, it's not a difficult journey, the buses stop in the town square, and if you get a direct service takes just over an hour. You can get buses from Siena to Volterra, changing at Colle but it's a longish journey so not feasible for a day trip.

Colle di Val d'Elsa and around

The rivers round here made Colle an early industrial town. Glass was produced from Roman times and in later centuries paper factories grew up. It's the place to come to buy crystal, both factory and handmade. There's a large shop in the lower part of town and a CALP factory on the outskirts. The town's divided in two: Colle Bassa, the workaday lower modern part, and Colle Alta, the medieval part up on the hill. There's a steep climb to the top from the lower square but it only takes 15 minutes. Once there you can mooch round the pretty streets and enjoy the views.

Sights

Museo Civico
Via del Castello, **T** 0577 923888. *Apr-Oct Tue-Sun 1030-1230, 1630-1930; Nov-end Mar, weekends only 1030-1230, 1530-1830. €3, €6 combined ticket with other town museums.*

Sienese and Florentine works of art spanning the 12th to the 20th centuries are on show in this museum. It includes a *Maestà* by a 12th- to 13th-century artist known as Maestro di Badia a Isola, created for a church near Monteriggione, and a rare eucharist vessel, the *Tesoro di Galgognano* from the 6th century. There are landscapes and illuminated manuscripts too.

Museo del Cristallo
Via dei Fossi 8, **T** 0577 934035. *Summer daily 1000-1200, 1600-1930, winter Tue-Sun. €3, €6 combined ticket with Museo Archeologico and Museo Civico.* See also p199

On the site of an old crystal factory, this museum tells you everything you've been dying to know about the history of crystal and its association with Colle. It shows tools and working techniques and has some fine crystal pieces.

Museo Archeologico
Piazza del Duomo 42, **T** 0577 922954. *May-Sep Tue-Sun 1000-1200, 1600-1900; Oct-Apr Tue-Fri 1530-1730, Sat, Sun 1000-1200, 1530-1830. €3.*

! Colle was the birthplace of Arnolfo di Cambio, the architect who designed Florence's Palazzo Vecchio.

Set in the old Palazzo Pretorio, recognized by all the coats of arms that cover the façade, this is a small collection of Etruscan finds from the area. They include exuberantly decorated vases.

● *Look for the Via delle Volte, it's a section of underground road built in medieval times when the townsfolk needed protection.*

Monteriggioni
About 10 km southeast of Colle di Val d'Elsa.

Small, but perfectly formed, best describes this medieval fortification that's as perfectly preserved as an ant in amber. It was built in 1203 by the Sienese to defend their northern border against the stroppy Florentines. A massive structure, it's easily seen from the road and instantly recognizable: a ring of walls studded with 14 towers. Dante mentions it in his *Inferno*, describing the towers as giants surrounding hell's abyss. The relevant quotation is carved on a plaque above the gate. Once inside there's a tiny hamlet with a church, hotel and restaurant.

★ San Gimignano

The towers that characterize this hilltop town have justly made it one of the most celebrated places in the world. Fourteen, out of an original 72, remain; stone skyscrapers that give the place a romantically menacing air. Unfortunately, a trip here is number one on everyone's Tuscan tick-list and visitors swarm here from around Easter to October. Sometimes it feels a bit like a living museum, the sort of place that everyone visits but where no one lives. To get the best from the town try and visit in the off-season, and stay overnight so you can get a better feel for its medieval charms once the day-trippers have left.

! While in San Gimignano try the local Vernaccia wine.

There are two types of combined ticket in San Gimignano: one gets you into all the civic museums. It costs €7.50. The other covers the Palazzo Communale, Pinacoteca and Torre Grossa and costs €5. The Collegiata is not included in either.

Sights

Collegiata

Piazza del Duomo, **T** 0577 940316. *Apr-Oct Mon-Fri 0930-1930, Sat 0930-1700, Sun 1230-1730; Nov-end Mar Mon-Sat 0930-1700, Sun 1230-1730, closed 21 Jan-end Feb. €3.50, €5.50 combined ticket with Museo d'Arte Sacra.*

Modelled on Siena's cathedral, with bold black and white stripes on the walls, this Romanesque collegiate church is simply covered with wonderfully lively frescoes. The **Cappella di Santa Fina**, a masterpiece of Renaissance architecture, contains works by Domenico Ghirlandaio, illustrating scenes from the life of the town's patron saint. The left aisle contains scenes from the *Old Testament* painted in the 1360s by Bartolo di Fredi, while the opposite wall tells the *New Testament* story, originally attributed to Barna da Siena, but now thought to be the work of La Bottega di Memmi. The panel portraying the creation of Adam and Eve is particularly charming. There are also two painted wooden statues by Jacopo della Quercia, and near the exit some particularly gruesome *Last Judgement* scenes by the Sienese painter Taddeo di Bartolo: *Inferno* and *Paradiso* are on opposing sides.

Palazzo Comunale

Piazza del Duomo, **T** 0577 990312. *Mar-Oct 0930-1900, Nov-end Feb 1000-1700. €5.*

> ### Towering ambition

Fortified houses were common in medieval Tuscany. Towns and families were often divided into Guelph and Ghibelline factions, and towers provided both a refuge and a place from which to bombard enemies. But they were also a status symbol – and everyone wanted a big one. Towers grew higher and higher as wealthy families tried to outdo one another. In the end it got out of hand and the authorities imposed a limit on their height. If a family fell out of favour, their tower would be demolished. After the Black Death, the population of San Gimignano fell and buildings began to be deserted and fall into disrepair. It became a sleepy backwater. Ironically this preserved the architecture: while more successful Tuscan towns were pulling down their towers, San Gimignano remained in a time warp. The town's tallest tower is the Torre Grossa, which soars over 60 m. If you're feeling energetic you can climb to the top for a panoramic view of the countryside. On a clear day they say you can see the Apuan Alps – just.

This medieval palace, beside the Collegiata, houses the **Museo Civico** and the **Pinacoteca**, and also gives you access to the **Torre Grossa** (see Towering ambition, above). The Sala di Dante, where Dante held a meeting with the local council, contains an almost exact copy of Simone Martini's *Maestà* in Siena's Palazzo Pubblico: it was done by his brother-in-law Lippo Memmi – but isn't as good. The Pinacoteca is filled with works by Tuscan and

! San Gimignano is known for the quality of its saffron, which has been cultivated here for centuries. It was so valuable that in medieval times the town council used it to pay a percentage of its debts.

Umbrian painters including Taddeo di Bartolo, Coppo di Marcovaldo, Pinturicchio and Filippino Lippi. The liveliest frescoes are in the **Camera del Podestà**; painted by Memmo di Filippuccio in the 14th century, they show a young married couple on their wedding night. One scene shows them in the bath together, another getting into bed.

Museo d'Arte Sacra
Piazza del Duomo. *€3.50, joint ticket with Collegiata €5.50.*

Devoted entirely to religious art, this small museum has items such as embroidered copes, chalices and paintings, including *The Madonna of the Rose*, part of a triptych by Bartolo di Fredi. There's an enormous throne from the late 15th century.
  ● *One of the best ways to enjoy the town is to take a walk along the quieter streets like Via Berignano, and around the walls. The views from the Rocca, the old fortress, are great.*

Chiesa Sant'Agostino
Piazza Sant'Agostino. *Nov-Mar 0700-1200, 1500-1800, Apr-Oct 0700-1200, 1500-1900. Free.*

In a quiet grassy square on the edge of the town, this church attracts fewer visitors but is worth the short walk. Built in the 13th century, it was later embellished with fine Renaissance frescoes. The high altar has a painting of the *Coronation of the Madonna* by Piero del Pollaiuolo, while the surrounding walls contain a fresco cycle filled with glimpses of 15th-century life; it depicts the *Life of St Augustine* and is the work of Benozzo Gozzoli and his pupils (1464-65). Take a look at the chapel dedicated to St Bartolo. It contains the saint's tomb, and terracotta flooring by Andrea della Robbia. To the left of the altar a door leads to a peaceful cloister, with roses and potted plants.

Museo Archeologico, Spezeria di Santa Fina and Galleria d'Arte Moderna
Via Folgore di San Gimignano, **T** 0577 940348. *1100-1730. €3.50.*

This is a strange mix of museums squeezed into one building. Downstairs there's a 13th-century pharmacy, moved from its original location in the city. You see the fragrant kitchen where potions were prepared. Other rooms contain archaeological exhibits including Etruscan pots and funerary urns. Upstairs you jump a few centuries to 19th- and 20th-century paintings, including landscapes and works by Giannetto Fieschi.

★ Volterra and around

Volterra feels distinctly different to other Tuscan towns. It's more isolated, perched on the edge of a sheer cliff, the Balze, and the landscape's wilder, hillier and more windswept. It's packed with reminders of its Etruscan and Roman past and is a good starting point for walks and drives. It's gradually becoming more fashionable – apparently George Clooney's just bought a house nearby.

Sights

Museo Etrusco Guarnacci
Via Don Minzoni 15, **T** 0588 86347. *Winter 0830-1345, summer 0900-1845. €7, combined ticket with Pinacoteca and Museo d'Arte Sacra.*

Volterra was one of the most important Etruscan cities and this fine – if old-fashioned – collection of artefacts gives a glimpse of that mysterious civilization (it's worth getting the audio guide). The ground floor shows how burial rituals became increasingly sophisticated. In pre-Etruscan times cinerary urns, holding the cremated body, had been essentially earthenware pots. In Etruscan times they were ornately carved: figures on top represented the deceased and gave a clue to their occupation, and there were also scenes of daily life and Greek mythology. No 136, for instance, shows a man holding a liver, indicating that he was a religious leader and would 'read' body organs.

The next floor covers later years and has a mix of Roman and Etruscan artefacts (the Etruscans were the first kings of Rome). The most important pieces are at either end: the *Urna degli Sposi*, the 1st-century funerary urn of an unflatteringly aged married couple, cuddled together on the ground. The man's middle fingers are bent, making a *sconguiro* sign – still used in some countries to ward off the evil eye.

At the other end is the *Ombra della Sera* (Shadow of the Evening), an elongated bronze statuette of a young boy with a slight pot belly from the 3rd century BC. Other exhibits include examples of *buccero* – unique ceramic work that's black inside and out. It's not known how they made it. The top floor contains more cinerary urns and items like mirrors, made from polished bronze.

Pinacoteca

Via dei Sarti 1, **T** 0588 87580. *Winter 0830-1345, summer 0900-1845. €7, combined ticket.*

Located in a Renaissance palace, attributed to Antonio Sangallo the Elder, this is the town's art gallery. The first floor includes a gilded polyptych by Taddeo di Bartolo of the *Madonna and Child with Saints* (1411) and two wooden sculptures of the *Annunciation* by the Sienese artist Francesco di Domenico Valdambrino. Highlights are a wood panel of the *Deposition*, signed and dated 1521 by Tuscan Mannerist painter Rosso Fiorentino, and one of

! Volterra's famous for its alabaster, a local white stone used by the Etruscans to make their funerary urns. The trade appeared to die out but was revived in the 18th century. You'll find it on sale all over the town.

Walks and drives around Volterra

Drive south of Volterra to explore a rougher, wilder country, and villages like **Pomarance**. There's the **Devil's Valley**, the eerie geo-thermic area where sulphurous jets of steam shoot from the earth. The town of **Larderello** was named after the man who began to extract boric acid from the broiling pools. And there are the **Colline Metallifere** or 'metal hills', exploited for centuries for their silver, copper, lead and zinc. Softer countryside is to the east in the **Val d'Elsa**, particularly south of the SR68, where there are pretty medieval villages like **Casole d'Elsa**, home to an impressive Collegiate church. There are plenty of possibilities for walks, including the woodlands of **Berignone** and **Monterufoli**, or the Castelvecchio reserve to the east. Ask the tourist office for information and get hold of a 1:25,000 map.

You could also try a climb up craggy **Monte Voltraio**. Start from **Villa Palagione** (off the SS439 near Volterra), turn left through the gates and after around 274 m go right at the red and white flash. Wind steeply uphill through the trees, past a sheer lookout point and continue to the top and the ruins of a fortified castle. Return on the track leading down to the right. It'll bring you to a crumbling 10th-century churchyard – exposed human bones are occasionally found, but there's no sign of their headstones. Continue past a stone building and back to the start.

Luca Signorelli's masterpieces, an *Annunciation* (1491) with brilliant, almost psychedelic colours. The second floor has works by Pier de Witte, and the top-floor gallery gives a panoramic view of the Roman Theatre.

Palazzo Viti

Via dei Sarti 41, **T** *0588 84047. Wed-Mon 0900-1300, 1430-1800, Tue 1430-1800, open by appointment only in winter. €4.*

Built in the 16th century by a local nobleman, this grand old palace later became the home of an alabaster merchant, Benedetto Giuseppe Viti, who made radical changes to the interior. The rooms are lavishly decorated with furniture, porcelain and alabaster.

● *The Porta all'Arco is the world's only standing Etruscan arch. A German general in the Second World War ordered his men to blow it up to impede the advance of the allies, but local people dug up the road in the night making access impossible.*

Roman Theatre

Off Viale Francesco Ferrucci, by the Porta Fiorentina. Summer daily 1030-1730, winter Sat and Sun 1100-1600 weekends.

Best viewed from Via Lungo le Mura al Mandorlo, and not to be confused with an amphitheatre, this is an impressively preserved Roman theatre, the second one they built in stone. Made in 10 BC it was dedicated to Augustus and seated a whopping 2,000 people. They had all mod cons: a goatskin covering to protect spectators from the rain and excellent acoustics. The seats were ranged in order of status, the glitterati getting the best, with the lower orders squeezed in at the top. You can also spot the remains of a sophisticated 3rd-century bath house, built partly with stones from the theatre. Citizens would come here for massages and toning rubs of olive oil and sand. The site was only rediscovered in the 1950s: prior to that it had been a rubbish dump and football pitch.

Palazzo dei Priori
Piazza dei Priori. *Mon-Fri (usually) 1000-1300, 1500-1900. €1.*

This 13th-century palace was Italy's first town hall, and it's still used today. The façade is covered with glazed coats of arms as well as the *canna volterrana*, the medieval standard measurement of the town. The Sala del Consiglio, the main hall, contains a large canvas of the *Marriage Feast at Cana*. The antechamber has a monochrome fresco, now on canvas, attributed to Luca Signorelli.

Duomo
Piazza San Giovanni. *Daily. Free.*

Consecrated in 1120, the façade is typically Pisan Romanesque style. The interior was much altered in the 16th century and the zebra stripes were done in the facist era of the 1930s. The pulpit's 12th century and there's an important painted wooden *Deposition* (1228) by an unknown artist. Unusually for the era, it depicts emotional, active figures – Nicodemus wields a pair of pliers, Joseph of Arimathea balances on a ladder and Christ is a suffering human, rather than triumphantly divine.

Churches in Volterra
Churches worth a visit include **San Francesco** (*by Porta San Francesco*), which features the Chapel of the Holy Cross, frescoed by Cenni di Francesco (1369-1415); **Chiesa San Michele** (*town centre*), a 13th-century church built on top of the old Roman forum; and on the edge of town, **San Giusto** (*15 mins' walk along Via Ricciarelli, through Porta San Francesco and ahead, no standard opening hours*), an unusual 17th-century church made of yellow stone. On sunny days, at midday, a ray of sunlight shines through a gnomonic hole and falls on to the marble meridian line on the floor.

Caporciano Mine and Museo delle Miniere

Mine, west of Volterra, 1 km from Montecatini Val di Cecina; **Museum**, Palazzo Pretorio, Piazza Garibaldi, Montecatini, **T** 347 8718870. *Easter-Nov, core times Thu, Sat and Sun 1600-1800; tours start at the mine on the hour, check beforehand as more tours may be available at busy times. €5, €3 for outside area only, €8 including museum in centre of the village.   See also p199*

Don hard hats for a guided tour of this old **copper mine**, built on a site once worked by the Etruscans. Once the largest copper mine in Europe it closed in 1907. An inscription above the entrance to the mine asks for God's protection for the workers. The tour follows a short section of tunnel and doesn't go deep down. Also on show are administrative offices, the enormous lift shaft known as Alfredo, and the wheel that drove it. The **museum** in the village incudes displays on salt mining (which brought wealth in the Middle Ages), alabaster and the area's geo-thermal history.

Abbazia di San Galgano

Southeast of Volterra on SS73, nearest village Palazzetto. *Abbey daily; chapel morning only. Free.*

This is one of Tuscany's most celebrated and most romantic spots, the ruined Cistercian abbey of San Galgano. It was built in the 12th century in honour of St Galgano, but was sacked in later years by *condottiere* Sir John Hawkwood, an Englishman who's commemorated on the interior of the Duomo in Florence. It gradually fell into ruin and was eventually deconsecrated. On the hill above is a chapel, built over the spot where Galgano had his hermitage. A dissolute knight, he had a revelation and came to live in this isolated spot and devote himself to prayer. In a reverse of the Arthurian legend he's said to have thrust his sword into a stone, symbolically renouncing worldly ways and forming the sign of the Cross. You can still see it – buried up to the hilt.

North of Siena

Chianti was once the promised land for the British. The landscape's craggy and hard to farm and, after the Second World War, local people had left in droves. From the 1960s the British middle classes began snapping up the ruined farmhouses that littered the countryside, buying them for just a few thousand pounds and converting them into fashionably rustic second homes – now worth small fortunes. Lured by the weather and the unspoilt countryside, many settled for good and were later followed by other foreigners chasing the Tuscan dream. It became known as 'Chiantishire', a term that still seems appropriate today, with British accents outnumbering Italian in some places. It's a favourite spot for honeymooners. Almost all the properties have now been restored – Sting's just one celebrity who's got an estate here; whole hamlets have been turned into hotels, and tourism is thriving. There are no more cheap properties and every undiscovered part of Italy is eagerly heralded as 'the new Chianti'. Charitably the Italians don't seem to resent this, shrugging and making the most of the region's new prosperity.

▸▸ *See Sleeping p117, Eating and drinking p144, Bars and clubs p158*

▸▸ *See Sleeping p117, Eating and drinking p144, Bars and clubs p158*

Chianti

What's great for visitors is that, although it's sprinkled with pretty villages, and has a generous share of castles and churches, there's nothing you feel obliged to see in the Chianti area – making it a pleasant antidote to treasure-filled cities like Siena. The countryside is entirely different to that of southern Tuscany. It's rugged, particularly in the northern 'Florentine Chianti', and full of oak, pine and chestnut woods. It's enough just to pootle off the beaten track following the network of unsurfaced strade bianchi *(white roads) that lace the countryside. Stop when you see something you like, have lazy lunches, and drop in to vineyards offering tastings of the local wine.*

The wine, of course, draws loads of visitors. The terrain that's so unsuited for ordinary agriculture is ideal for growing grapes, and farmers are rushing back to the land. Chianti Classico is a DOCG wine, a long way from the plonk once sold in raffia-wrapped bottles and later turned into a nifty lamp. The S222, the main route that cuts the region north to south, is generally known as the chiantigiana, *and forms a natural wine route. Exploring by public transport really isn't an option; you need a car to get about. Alternatively, go by bike; the* strade bianchi *make great cycle trails. The main centres fill up in the summer, while spring and autumn are quieter, cooler and more colourful. Go at harvest time for instance, late October to early December, and you could find fresh* porcini *on the menu, newly pressed olive oil on the table, hills turned gold with autumn leaves and the scent of woodsmoke lingering in the air.*

Sights

Quercegrossa
Close to Siena, this unassuming village is mainly known as the birthplace of the great sculptor Jacopo della Quercia (c1367-1438). On the main road, **Santi Giacomo e Niccolò** church contains a late 15th-century painted wood *Pietà*, by Franceso di Giorgio Martini, that's recently been restored.

Castellina in Chianti
One of the most important centres in Chianti, Castellina is a bustling hill town with a historic fortress in the centre and an Etruscan tomb on the outskirts. It's an excellent base, with some good places to eat and drink and medieval streets in which to wander. **Via delle Volte** is an underground street with tiny secret hideouts and cellars – a legacy of more turbulent times. The surrounding countryside is full of atmospheric old farmhouses. You can hire bikes from the tourist office and, with notice, they'll find you a walking guide.

Radda in Chianti

Generally known as the capital of Chianti, Radda is a well-preserved hill village bearing the remains of ancient fortifications. It's got a great *gelateria*, Sandy, and several bars and restaurants. The **Palazzo del Podestà**, its façade covered with coats of arms, is due to open to the public (though no date as yet). On the first floor there's a fresco of the Florentine school (16th century) that's recently been restored. **San Niccolò** church is medieval, but has an unusual Liberty-style façade after it was rebuilt at the turn of the 20th century. There's a medieval wooden crucifix inside.

Volpaia

An ancient fortified village high in the hills, Volpaia was traditionally Florentine. It's hard to distinguish the village from the castle, they're essentially the same. You find low arches in the street, built to thwart assailants on horses, and the cemetery is inside the castle. It was on the Via Francigena and pilgrims would stop here on their way to Rome. Look above the door of **Casa Selvolini** and you can make out a square cross in the stone – the sign of the Knights of Malta.

Gaiole in Chianti

The village started life as a market place and hasn't grown much since. It's not far from two imposing castles. **Castello di Cacchiano** (**T** 0577 747018, cacchiano@chianticlassico.com) is an 11th-century Florentine fort that has panoramic views from the terrace – you can see the Val d'Orcia and the peak of Monte Amiata, Tuscany's highest peak. It's been producing wine for 500 years and now offers tastings and tours of the cellars (*Tue-Sat, morning and afternoon; best to call first*). From the terrace you can see the **Castello di Brolio** (**T** 0577 730220, www.castellitoscani.com/brolio; *gardens Mon-Fri 0900-1200, 1430-1700, Sun 0900-1200, 1430-1730, €3*), one of Chianti's main attractions. Another early Florentine fortress, it's the seat of the powerful Ricasole family, one of the major wine producers, and was where Baron Bettino Ricasole created the *Chianti Classico* wine formula. A cypress-lined drive leads to a gate in an enormous wall. The sign outside asks you to ring the door pull and someone will come and let you in. You can visit the castle, gardens and church. For tours and tastings make a reservation.

Castelnuovo Berardenga

The closest of the Chianti towns to Siena, this was another fortified village. It is now surrounded by soft vine-studded countryside, full of immaculately restored villas and pots spilling over with scarlet geraniums. The church in the main square contains a *Madonna and Child with Angels* by Giovanni di Paolo (1426). It's also the site of the **Villa Chigi** (**T** 0577 355500, *Sun 1000-1700 winter, 1000-2000 summer, free*), the home of the founder of Siena's musical academy. The gardens are the main draw.

East of Siena

As you move east from Siena you reach the more commercial, industrialized area, traversed by the A1 *autostrada* that links Rome to the north. A 90-minute bus journey takes you to Arezzo, the springboard for a trail of works by Piero della Francesca, the acclaimed Renaissance painter who was born in nearby Sansepolcro and spent most of his life in this area.

From Arezzo you can get a bus or train to Cortona, a neat and pretty town with Etruscan origins, picturesque buildings and Juliet-style balconies. Set on a hill that rises sharply from the reclaimed marshes of the Valdichiana, the steep, winding streets make for energetic strolls.

▸▸ *See Sleeping p120, Eating and drinking p148, Bars and clubs p158*

★ Arezzo

Arezzo is a prosperous working town, the lower part busy and modern, the upper part well tended and medieval. Once a month the town gets full to bursting with Italians, attracted by the large antique market that spills out of the main square into the surrounding streets. It's fun if you want to experience local life, but best avoided if you're on an artistic pilgrimage as it's frustratingly hard to move around.

◉ Sights

San Francesco
Piazza San Francesco, **T** 0575 24001. *Mon-Fri winter 0900-1800 summer 0900-1900, Sat 0900-1530, Sun 1300-1730. Entry to the frescoes on the hour and half hour, €6 tickets need to be reserved in high season; booking office is next to the church; church free.*

This huge Franciscan church is most people's first stop in Arezzo. The walls are covered with fragments of frescoes which were painted as a sort of 'bible of the poor', making the Christian story accessible to the illiterate. There's a huge wooden crucifix over the altar, the work of an Umbrian artist, and behind the altar are Piero della Francesca's frescoes illustrating the *Legend of the True Cross*. To get a proper look at them you need to buy a ticket. They had been badly damaged by damp and it took 15 years – and a great deal of money – to restore them. The panels don't follow a narrative order but are arranged to be most aesthetically appealing – structure, symmetry and geometry were important to him. The story starts at the top with Adam's death – a seed planted on his grave growing into the tree that made the Cross. One of the most famous panels is on the back wall, bottom right, in which King Constantine has a dream where an angel tells him that he would beat his enemies by giving up his weapons and fighting under the sign of the Cross. It's the first night scene by an Italian painter. Panels on the other side wall include one in which a man is dropped down a well to force him to say where the Cross is buried; and one in which, out of three possibilities, the true cross is discovered when it resurrects a dead man. The last one, at the top of this wall, shows the Cross going back to Jerusalem.

Piazza Grande

The town's medieval piazza is an unusual trapezoidal shape, with a distinct slope. On one side is a 16th-century arched loggia designed by Vasari, essentially the first shopping mall, with swish apartments above and shops underneath. It was reserved for the wealthy. A sign remains reminding members of the lower orders that they'd be subjected to the local equivalent of the stocks if they were found under the hallowed arches. Now some smart restaurants mingle with antique shops which, along with those on Via di Seteria, look like antiques themselves.

Backing on to the piazza is the **Pieve Santa Maria** (*0900-1300, 1500-1800, free*), entrance from Corso d'Italia. Built in the 12th century, it was originally the town's cathedral. Steps by the altar lead to the choir where there's a painted cross (1262) and a polyptych by Pietro Lorenzetti (1320). The façade has three tiers of columns, which get progressively closer and smaller. Some, in an early example of recycling, are Roman. Sculptures above the door show scenes from each month of year – May is represented by soldiers going to war; apparently it was the favoured time.

● *To the side, in Via di Seteria, you can see a door which has part of a 9th-century church above it. Look carefully among the geometric shapes and you can see the face of Christ on top, with his fingers in the level below, and his toes peeping out below that.*

Duomo

Piazza del Duomo, **T** 0575 23991. *Early-1230; 1500-1900. Free.*

Although it was started in 1277, work carried on for centuries, and the bell tower wasn't completed until 1936. It's noted for its stained-glass windows (1516-1525) by a French Dominican friar Guillaume de Marsillait. They're distinctive with architectural backgrounds, bright colours and flesh tones of the people's faces. In one, depicting Christ driving the money lenders out of the temple, there's a man in a red hat who seems to be running straight at you, no matter where you stand. Near the tomb of Pope Gregory is a small fresco of *Mary Magdalene* (1460) by Piero della Francesca in which he demonstrates his knowledge of perspective. She's holding an opaque apothecary's jar – a local tradition always depicts her as a bearer of myrrh. The church also contains the ornate tomb of San Donato. A neighbouring column, topped with an oil lamp, is said to be the one on which he was beheaded.

● *If you're in the mood for shopping make for* **Corso Italia**, *the main street. It's lined with clothes shops, including* Sugar, *which stocks designer goods for men and women. You'll find* Dolce e Gabbana *and* Prada. *But if bling's your thing you'll be disappointed. Although Arezzo's the centre of Italian gold production there are few jewellers in the city – most of the work goes on in factories out of town.*

La Casa Museo di Ivan Bruschi

Corso Italia 14, **T** 0575 900404. *Tue-Sun 1000-1300, 1500-1900. €3.*

The home of a famous antiquarian that houses his enormous collection of antiques and oddities from around the world. It's spread over three floors and contains everything from Etruscan urns to African statues. There are displays of his stamps (neatly arranged in patterns and stuck into books), household items, glassware, books and gold coins.

San Domenico
Piazza San Domenico. *Daily. Free.*

Famous for a crucifix (1260-65) by Cimabue, Giotto's teacher, San Domenico at first looks Byzantine, but then you see the hint of muscles in the body and the blood, coming from the wounds, realistically coagulating. A few drops even fall onto the golden frame.

Museo Archeologico
Via Margaritone 10, **T** 0575 20882. *0830-1930. €4.*

On the edge of town, next to the Roman amphitheatre, the museum contains important finds including a vase attributed to the Greek painter Euphronius.

Fortezza Medicea
Viale Bruno Buozzi. *Daily. Free.*

Not far from the Duomo, a public park leads to this fortress. It was built in the 16th century by the Florentines who destroyed houses, churches and lanes in the process. It's generally quiet and gives good views of the town and the distant mountain. If you want to picnic in the *fortezza* you'll find a couple of nice bread shops at the junction of Corso d'Italia and Via di Seteria; there's a good cheese shop opposite.

Monterchi and Sansepolcro

Art lovers will think they've died and gone to heaven in these villages. Unassuming Monterchi has a stunning painting of a pregnant Madonna, created by Piero della Francesca who was born at Sansepolcro, where you can see more examples of his work in the Museo Civico.

Sights

Madonna del Parto Museum

Via Reglia 1, Monterchi, *T* 0575 70713. *Tue-Sun summer 0900-1300, 1400-1900, winter 0900-1300, 1400-1800. €3.10, combination ticket with Sansepolcro museums €12.*

A rather dilapidated former school in a small village is the home of one of the most unusual paintings in western art: Piero della Francesca's *Madonna del Parto* (1450-1468). It depicts Mary while pregnant, with angels parting the curtains around her as if she's on a stage. The church used to disapprove of such a human depiction of the Madonna, but they've come round to the idea now. Some think it was a homage to the artist's mother, who was born in Monterchi. The angels are wearing red and green – the colours of the town. The painting used to be in a church in the town and was later moved elsewhere – no one seems quite sure where. It was recently restored at a cost of over €100,000, and is now displayed alone in a glass case. Other rooms are given over to detailed descriptions of its restoration. The painting has become a point of pilgrimage and women hoping to have a child will often come here to pray before it.

Museo Civico

Via Niccolò Aggiunti 65, Sansepolcro, **T** 0575 732218. *Oct-May 0930-1300, 1430-1800; Jun-Sep 0930-1330, 1430-1930. €6.20. Combination tickets (€12) for the Museo Civico and Aboca Museum in Sansepolcro, and Madonna del Parto in Monterchi are available from the Tourist Office on Via Matteotti, **T** 0575 740536.*

The town was the birthplace of Piero della Francesca (1415-1492) and the former town hall is now a museum, with some celebrated examples of his work. There's the *Madonna della Misericordia* (1445-1461), an early polyptych, richly gilded and displaying his distinctive geometric forms. There's also a fresco of the *Resurrection of Christ* (1458-74) which depicts Christ in a landscape with his foot resting on a battlement; soldiers sleep beneath him one of whom, dressed in brown, is said to resemble the artist. Aldous Huxley once declared it the greatest painting in the world. Other works include a ceramic of the *Nativity* by della Robbia: look closely and you'll see that it was done as a 'jigsaw'.

Aboca Museum

Via Niccolò Aggiunti 75, Sansepolcro, **T** 0575 733 589.
Oct-Mar Tue-Sun 1000-1300, 1430-1800; Apr-Sep 1000-1300, 1500-1900. €8.

A former palace that's been turned into a fragrant museum of herbalism – a pleasant change if you've had your fill of high culture. There are carefully illustrated old herb books, huge majolica storage jars, masses of dried herbs, an old apothecary's shop and a 'poison cell', where toxic remedies were tucked behind an iron grill. Make sure to walk round with one of the informative brochures, as labelling's in Italian.

Duomo

Via Matteotti, Sansepolcro. *Daily. Free.*

The cathedral contains a gilded polyptych of the *Resurrection* (14th century), attributed to Niccolò di Segna; the central figure of Christ stands in a pose so similar to Piero della Francesca's in the Museo Civico, that many feel Piero must have studied this first. There's also 10th-century carving of *Christ on the Cross*.

Cortona

There are enough museums and works of art in Cortona to occupy you for a couple of days at least – Fra Angelico and Luca Signorelli are the stars. It's also a good base for exploring the villages of the Valdichiana and nearby Lago Trasimeno. However, it's much more commercialized than Arezzo. It's been besieged by visitors ever since American author Frances Mayes set up home here and wrote about her experiences in Under the Tuscan Sun, *now a film. Late spring and summer are particularly busy. Not all the locals approve of visitors on this modern literary trail. They did, as one said, 'have Fra Angelico long before Frances Mayes'.*

Sights

Museo dell'Accademia Etrusca

Palazzo Casali, Piazza Signorelli 9, **T** 0575 637235. *Tue-Sun Nov-Mar 1000-1700, Apr-Oct 1000-1900. €4.20. To visit the tombs ask at the museum or* **T** *0575 630415.*

You can't miss the prize exhibit here: an Etruscan bronze oil lamp (4th century BC) hanging from the ceiling of its own little temple. It was probably designed for an important sanctuary and looks much like a chandelier. It's covered with ornate carvings of goddesses and priapic satyrs. The rest of the room is filled with cases displaying serried ranks of Etruscan bronzes – all the more mysterious because they're not labelled. There are tiny swaddled babies, horses, a delicately worked swan and mice nibbling at ears of corn. At the end are paintings by Luca Signorelli and his nephew.

The remainder of the rooms are filled with everything from Egyptian artefacts – including a wooden funerary boat – to Tuscan paintings. On the top floor are finds from **Melone del Sodo**, the Etruscan tomb just outside the town. They include an exquisite gold panther and delicate jewellery. A scale model of the tomb gives some idea of its sophistication.

▶ Fra Angelico

Fra Angelico is one of the most celebrated of the early Renaissance artists. Born Guido di Pietro c1387, he became a Dominican friar in 1407, together with his brother. A talented artist, influenced by Giotto, his works were meant to stimulate prayer and meditation. He prayed before starting work and his paintings are notable for their tenderness and glorious colours. John Ruskin once said he was ' not an artist…[but] an inspired saint'. He spent four years in Cortona, and worked all over Tuscany as well as in Rome. Known in Italy as Beato Angelico (the 'blessed' Angelico) he died in 1455 and is buried in Rome.

Museo Diocesano

Piazza del Duomo, **T** 0575 62830. *Tue-Sun, Apr-Oct 1000-1900, Nov-Mar 1000-1700.* €5.

Made out of two former churches, this museum contains some stunning works of art. Behind the former altar of one church is Fra Angelico's superbly delicate *Annunciation* (c1430), done when he lived in Cortona for a few years. A Dominican friar, it was said that tears would pour down his face as he painted. Other artists represented include Sassetta, Pietro Lorenzetti and, in a downstairs gallery, Luca Signorelli. Twentieth-century works by Gino Severini line the stairs.

! "When I saw this work, I nearly fainted dead from shock and love of it. I could not have done it alone. I sighed and wept." (Fra Angelico, on the *Annunciation* in the Museo Diocesano)

San Domenico
By Piazza Garibaldi. *Daily but sometimes closed. Free.*

The sun's fading one of this Gothic church's most precious items: a lunette above the door frescoed by Fra Angelico (c 1433-34). Inside is a 16th-century altarpiece by Luca Signorelli.

Santa Margherita
Piazzale Santa Margherita, **T** 0575 603116. *Winter 0830-1200, 1500-1800, summer 0730-1200, 1500-1930. Free.*

There's been a church on this site since 1297, built in honour of St Margaret of Cortona. The present church was built in the 19th century. It's got an eye-catching blue ceiling and a rose window made by Giovanni Pisano. In pride of place is the intact body of St Margaret, set in a glass coffin. Should you wish you can press a switch to light it up.

● *You can walk to the church from Cortona by following the Viale Santa Margherita. It joins an ancient track, possibly used by medieval pilgrims, along which are the Stations of the Cross decorated with mosaics by the artist Gino Severini.*

Convento delle Celle
3.5 km east of Cortona, **T** 0575 603362, www.lecelle.it. *0830-1200, 1530-1830. Free.*

Set in a peaceful hollow beside a gushing stream, this monastery was built by St Francis in 1211 and enlarged over the centuries. Built in creamy stone on the craggy slopes of Monte Sant'Egidio, it's immensely evocative. You can visit the original chapel and St Francis' tiny cell, with its wooden bed and wooden pillow. St Francis used to stop here regularly on his travels and visited just four months before he died in 1226.

Frantoio Landi

Loc Cegliolo 71, Mezzavia, **T** 0575 612814. *A 15-min drive from Cortona.*

If you fancy some olive oil take a trip out to Frantoio Landi, a family-run olive oil mill. Olives are collected and pressed between granite stones in the traditional way – they'll give you a tour of the factory – and in season (November/December) you can watch the pressing. The family's own oil is for sale.

The city walls mean that Siena just can't expand to accommodate all the tourists who want to stay here in high season, so you need to book well in advance. The busiest times are around the Palio – 2 July and 16 August – Easter, and from late August to early October when the floors of the Duomo are uncovered. There's a very limited choice of good central hotels. Medieval buildings inevitably mean rooms that are small and often dark, and impressive reception areas often conceal rooms filled with uninspiring assortments of furniture and dingy bathrooms. However, staying in the centre is the best way of experiencing Siena's atmosphere, and it means that you can visit all the sights on foot. The newest, most spacious hotels with swimming pools are on the city's outskirts. But although they're often quieter, they can be bland. A few places offer bed and breakfast, and self-catering is also an attractive option whether in central apartments or in one of the burgeoning number of *agriturismi* – converted farms and villas in the countryside.

€ **Sleeping codes**

Price			
LL	€ 300 and over	C	€ 75-99
L	€ 250-299	D	€ 50-74
AL	€ 200-249	E	€ 35-49
A	€ 150-199	F	€ 25-34
B	€ 100-149	G	€ 24 and under

Prices are for a double room in high season. Self-catering properties are not coded as prices vary enormously with the season, number of guests and length of stay.

Terzo di San Martino

Hotels

B Hotel Antica Torre, Via di Fieravecchia 7, **T** 0577 222255, www.anticatorresiena.it. *Map 2, C11, p237* Breakfast not included. An ancient tower (hence the name) dating back to the 16th century, this hotel's as tall and narrow as you'd expect. Rooms and bathrooms are small but clean, with floaty curtains and marble floors. They're furnished simply and the whitewashed walls are dotted with photos and prints, while the ceilings have thick wooden beams. Steep stone stairs run down to a tiny breakfast room deep in the bowels of the building; it was once a pottery but feels a little like a prison cell.

B Hotel Santa Caterina, Via ES Piccolomini 7, **T** 0577 221105, www.hscsiena.it. *15-20 mins' walk from the Campo. Map 1, L8, p235* There's a real home-from-home feel at this lovely hotel just outside the city walls. The staff are consistently friendly and helpful, and about half the rooms overlook a gorgeous Tuscan valley. Breakfast is excellent with fresh fruit juices, pastries, rolls, cheeses, meat and plenty of fruit and yoghurt. In summer you can have it in the pretty little garden; in winter in the conservatory.

B-C Piccolo Hotel Oliveta, Via ES Piccolomini 35, **T** 0577 283930, www.oliveta.com. *A couple of mins' walk from the Porta Romana. Map 1, L8, p235* This is a former farmhouse next door to the hotel Santa Caterina. It's got a fresh, rustic feel and friendly staff. All 12 rooms are slightly different but have pastel wallpaper, cheery bedcovers and plenty of light. Many of the smaller rooms have lovely views across the valley. There's a good choice for breakfast and a relaxing atmosphere.

Bed and breakfast

D Casa Laura, Via Roma 3, **T** 0577 226061, casalaurasiena@ libero.it. *Not far from the Porta Romana. Map 2, E12, p237* Laura's house: just four clean, simple rooms in an upstairs apartment. Worth considering if you're on a budget.

Terzo di Città

Hotels

A-B Palazzo Ravizza, Pian dei Mantellini 34, **T** 0577 280462, www.palazzoravizza.it. *Map 2, G1, p236* In a quiet corner of the Contrada della Pantera (Panther), this former Renaissance palace is now an elegant hotel run by the Grottanelli de'Santi family. Some rooms have views of the surrounding countryside and many are decorated with frescoes. Antiques are dotted around and the public areas have comfy chairs, newspapers and ornate coffered ceilings. Best of all is the tranquil garden where you can have tea or relax with a book. Breakfast is taken outside in summer. The hotel has its own parking – a rare perk in the city centre.

B Hotel Duomo, Via Stalloreggi 38, **T** 0577 289088, www.hotelduomo.it. *Map 2, E3, p236* The magnificent stone staircase in this hotel is a distinctive reminder of the building's origins as a 12th-century *palazzo*. Furniture in many of the rooms tends to have more of a 1970s feel, although those on the top floor are fresher with cream wood furniture and light green/cream decor. Request a room with a view when you're booking. Some, such as No 54, have a panoramic view of the nearby Duomo, whereas a few downstairs have no view but modern furnishings.

Bed and breakfast

B-D Residenza d'Epoca Il Casato, Via Giovanni Duprè 126 and Via Casato di Sopra, **T** 0577 236001, www.hotelrooms.it/ilcasato. *Map 2, F5, p236* 12 rooms and an apartment in this quirky 14th-century building. Only an option for those who can cope with very steep steps. Rooms can be dark but some have ornate painted ceilings and some have a balcony. There's a pretty terraced garden too.

Terzo di Camollia

Hotels

LL Grand Hotel Continental, Via Banchi di Sopra 85, **T** 0577 56011, www.royaldemeure.com. *Map 3, E9, p239* Suitably plum location on Siena's smartest street for this swish five-star hotel with 51 rooms. Once a rich family's villa, it's now been restored with exuberant frescoes and lashings of gilt. Room 138 has a terrace, and suite 135 offers the best view of the Palio parade. One for honeymoons and special occasions.

B-C Hotel Chiusarelli, Viale Curtatone 15, **T** 0577 280562, www.chiusarelli.com. *Map 3, E6, p238* Probably best for footie fans as it backs onto the local stadium. With a busy road on the other side it's certainly not a peaceful option; stadium-side rooms are quietest (unless it's a match day). Rooms don't live up to the grand marble entrance hall, being functional rather than plush, but they're clean and have newly tiled bathrooms. Handy for the bus station, under five minutes' walk away, and close to San Domenico church.

C Albergo Cannon D'Oro, Via dei Montanini 28, **T** 0577 44321, www.cannondoro.com. *Map 3, C9, p239* No hiding if you've over-indulged on pasta: the corridors of this two-star hotel are dotted with unforgiving full-length mirrors. Rooms are filled with a mish-mash of furniture and have plain whitewashed walls. No frills but it's clean and reasonably central.

C Hotel La Toscana, Via Cecco Angiolieri 12, **T** 0577 46097, **F** 0577 270634. *Map 3, F10, p239* Spread over five floors in a 13th-century house, this three-star hotel has 40 uninspired but clean rooms – some with functional modern furniture, others with dark wood and older bathrooms. The public areas have a grander, medieval feel with wrought-iron chandeliers and arched ceilings. Convenient for the Campo and the shops. Breakfast is extra.

C Piccolo Hotel Etruria, Via delle Donzelle, 3, **T** 0577 288088, www.hoteletruria.com. *One min's walk from the Campo. Map 3, G10, p239* This friendly family-run hotel, bang in the centre of the city, offers excellent value. The 20 simply furnished rooms have tiled floors and functional fittings, and everything is spotlessly clean. There's also a very pleasant area where guests can sit and relax. Breakfast costs an extra €5.

Bed and breakfast

C-D Albergo Bernini, Via della Sapienza 15, **T** 0577 289047, www.albergobernini.com. *Map 3, E7, p239* Italian hotels have a tendency to have glorious façades that too frequently conceal dingy rooms. This B&B turns that concept on its head with an uninspiring entrance but nine clean, well-maintained rooms and lovely views of the city. Owned by the Saracini family, it has a relaxed atmosphere and central location. Fittings are old and in some rooms you might have to share a bathroom, but it's good value. Great views of the Duomo from rooms 10 and 11. Breakfast on the balcony in summer.

D Alma Domus, Via Camporegio 37, **T** 0577 44177. *Map 3, F6, p238* This former convent still has a slightly regimented atmosphere – there's a 2330 curfew and you half expect a cry of 'stand by your beds' in the morning. The 56 rooms run off long corridors and are simply furnished but clean, and some have a view over the city. It's convenient for San Domenico and Casa Santa Catarina.

D-E Albergo Tre Donzelle, Via delle Donzelle 5, **T** 0577 280358, **F** 0577 223933. *Map 3, F11, p239.* Situated in an ancient building, this is the oldest hotel in Siena and it's in need of modernization, with 27 plain rooms and worn furniture. There are no TVs in the rooms nor is there air conditioning, however, it's clean and is extremely close to the Campo, so is worth considering for those on a budget who want to be right in the heart of things. The cheapest rooms have shared bathrooms.

Serviced apartments

Palazzo Piccolomini, Via Sallustio Bandini 35, **T** 055 244456, www.florencerentals.net. *Map 3, F12, p239* On the top floor of a 16th-century building close to the Campo, are these four good-quality serviced apartments with lots of original features like tiled terracotta floors, plus new washing machines and good kitchens. One sleeps four to five, the rest two to three. The flats can work out cheaper than a hotel and you'll feel as if you're a real resident of the city. (From €1,273 per week, minimum rental one week, reduced rate for longer stays.)

Outskirts of Siena

Hotels

LL Hotel Certosa di Maggiano, Strada di Certosa 82, **T** 0577 288180, www.certosadimaggiano.com. *Southeast of the city. Map 1, L8, p235 (off map)* Built in the 14th century, this former monastery is the last word in luxury – it even has a heli-pad. The great and good come here; it's beautifully secluded with a swimming pool, olive trees and lovely gardens, and is – just – within walking distance of the city. Nothing monastic about the rooms or the service – very, very classy.

LL Park Hotel Siena, Via di Marciano 18, **T** 0577 290290, www.royaldemeure.com. *Northwest of Siena. (Off map)* This old villa is the sister to the Grand Hotel Continental in the city centre. The public areas have lots of medieval-style features and rooms have good-sized beds and lots of rich colours. There's a pool, tennis courts and a small golf course, but unless you've got a car you'll probably be reliant on taxis to get in and out of Siena.

A Frances' Lodge, Strada di Valdipugna, **T** 0577 281061, www.franceslodge.it. *A couple of kilometres east of Siena. (Off map)* Farmhouse in a peaceful location with vineyards, olive groves and a pretty garden. The rooms are decorated in different colours and styles – from sleek whites to warm spice shades. The lodge has a small pool and serves good breakfasts with home-made jams and marmalades.

B Hotel Garden, Via Custoza 2, **T** 0577 47056, www.gardenhotel.it. *Map 1, A1, p234 (off map)* This large hotel just on the northern edge of the city is a very good bet for families as there are two swimming pools, a tennis court and pleasant gardens – you can spot red squirrels if you get up early. Only 26 rooms in the original, rather elegant, villa; others are in newer blocks, the best being in Belvedere. Lots of frescoes in the villa, good choice for breakfast and a pleasant, relaxed atmosphere. Buses stop nearby for the centre.

Self-catering

B-D Villa Agostoli, Strada degli Agostoli 99, **T** 0577 44392, www.gardenhotel.it. *Just under 5 km west of the city. (Off map)* If you've got a car these lovely self-catering villas and apartments are worth a try. Set among olive and pomegranate trees and with a swimming pool, they sleep from two to eight people, are very attractively furnished with well-equipped kitchens and their own patios. Rentals are weekly (from €985 high season) and prices vary seasonally.

Hostels

G Ostello Guidoriccio, Via Fiorentina 85, **T** 0577 52212, siena.aighostel@virgilio.it. *About 1 km northwest of the city centre. (Off map)* Around 100 beds at this budget youth hostel. Rooms are all shared and you'll need to use the bus to get into Siena. Only for those really strapped for cash.

South of Siena

Montepulciano

A Fattoria Martiena, Via di Martiena 8, just outside Montepulciano, **T** 0578 716905, www.martiena.it. *Closed Jan-early Feb.* Country-style bed and breakfast in a former olive oil mill. Rooms have quirky shapes and features; there are open fires and a terrace where you can have breakfast on fine days.

B Albergo Duomo, Via San Donato 14, **T** 0578 757473, www.albergoduomo.it. Family-run hotel, right opposite the town's cathedral. Beamed ceilings and simple furnishings. The largest rooms are on the first floor.

B-C Il Borghetto, Via Borgo Buio 7, **T** 0578 757535. Each of the 15 rooms is different in this friendly, family-run hotel, but all of them are clean, have private bathrooms and contain unusual antique furniture – one room has a Neapolitan bed inlaid with mother-of-pearl. Some rooms have a superb view of the surrounding countryside, and there's a sitting room with a huge old fireplace. Pets are accepted but breakfast is not provided.

Pienza

A-B Hotel Relais, Il Chiostro, Corso Il Rossellino 26, **T** 0578 748400, www.relaisilchiostrodipienza.com. Beautifully converted 15th-century convent in central Pienza. Lots of atmosphere with quiet cloisters, comfortable rooms and a good restaurant.

C Albergo Rutiliano, Via della Madonnina 18, **T** 0578 749408, www.albergorutiliano.it. Polished wooden floors, simple

West of Siena

Colle di Val d'Elsa and around

AL Hotel Monteriggioni, Via Maggio 4, Monteriggioni, **T** 0577 305009, www.hotelmonteriggioni.net. *About halfway beteween Siena and Colle di Val d'Elsa.* This is the only hotel in this tiny hilltop hamlet, but it's worth considering if you want a quiet base that's also convenient for visiting other sights. There are just 12 rooms which are small but attractive, with black and white tiled bathrooms. There's a little garden and a pool too.

D Villa Sabolini, Loc Mensanello, **T** 0577 972001, www.villasabolini.com. *South of Colle di Val d'Elsa.* Bed and breakfast in a grand, old villa that has basic, clean and simply furnished rooms ideal for families or anyone looking for cheap but decent accommodation. Often caters for groups.

Tenuta di Mensanello, **T** 0577 971080, www.mensanello.com. *5 km south of Colle di Val d'Elsa.* Clean and simple apartments to rent on a farm estate.

San Gimignano

LL-L La Collegiata, Loc Strada 27, **T** 0577 943201, www.collegiata.it. *A short drive northwest from San Gimignano.* A long driveway leads to this exclusive former convent that dates back to 1587 – it's the choice of the rich and famous. Staying here is a bit like relaxing in your own private villa. Rooms are luxurious, there's a lovely swimming pool and the restaurant's excellent. Be prepared to bump into Tony Blair.

B L'Antico Pozzo, Via San Matteo 87, **T** 0577 942014, www.anticopozzo.com. Plenty of history at this town house which dates back to the Middle Ages – there's still a well inside. In the 18th-century wild society parties were held here. It's less decadent today but still atmospheric, with frescoes and four-poster beds in some rooms – others are more modern.

B-C Bel Soggiorno, Via San Giovanni 91, **T** 0577 940375, www.hotelbelsoggiorno.it. Comfortable three-star hotel, with inoffensively decorated rooms and a reasonably priced restaurant. Three rooms have a terrace – worth requesting as the view is great.

C Leon Bianco, Piazza della Cisterna, **T** 0577 941294, www.leonbianco.com. You couldn't get a more convenient base than this established, family-run hotel in the village's main square. About half the rooms have views over the surrounding countryside – they're more expensive than those that overlook the square. There's an attractive terrace where the breakfast buffet is served on fine days. Potted plants dotted around, tiled floors and simply furnished but clean and comfortable rooms.

C Locanda La Mandragola, Via Diaccceto 7, **T** 0577 940454, www.locandalamandragola.it. Cosy bed and breakfast down a side street. The furniture's worn but the rooms are clean and about half have views (specify when you book). There's a little garden too. A few narrow stairs take you to a tiny rooftop terrace with a couple of seats and panoramic views.

Volterra and around

B Park Hotel Le Fonti, Via di Fontecorrenti, **T** 0588 85219, www.parkhotellefonti.com. Large, modern four-star hotel with swimming pool, a terrace that has good views, and comfortable rooms with tiled floors. Some suites available.

B-C La Locanda, Via Guarnacci 24/28, **T** 0588 81547,
www.hotel-lalocanda.com. Four-star hotel conveniently situated
within the town walls. Comfortably furnished rooms with marbled
tiled bathrooms and cable TV.

C Albergo Villa Nencini, Borgo Santo Stefano 55, **T** 0588 86386,
www.villanencini.it. This hotel outside the town walls has 35
rather bland rooms, although many have good views and there's
a large swimming pool and a restaurant, so it's a decent option
for anyone with kids in tow.

C Nazionale, Via dei Marchesi 11, **T** 0588 86284,
www.albergonazionalevolterra.it. Convenient, central
location and bland, but clean modern rooms at this three-star
hotel. DH Lawrence stayed here while writing *Etruscan Places*.
Seven rooms have a balcony – well worth requesting as the
views are great.

C Villa Porta all'Arco, Via Mazzini 2, **T** 0588 81487,
www.villaportallarco.it. *Just outside the Etruscan gate to
Volterra*. This hotel looks a bit impersonal on the outside,
but has charming, old-fashioned interiors with clean, simple
furnishings in the rooms. Parking's available and it's a
15-minute walk up into Volterra.

C Villa Rioddi, Strada Provinciale Monte Volterrano, Loc Rioddi,
T 0588 88053, www.hotelvillarioddi.it. *About 3 km southwest from
Volterra*. Lovely country-style interiors at this small (15 rooms)
hotel – a 15th-century villa out in the country. Very clean and
comfortable with expansive views and a delightfully situated
swimming pool.

D La Primavera, Via Porta Diana 15, **T** 0588 87295,
www.affittacamere-laprimavera.com. *10 mins' walk from the town*

centre. Just five rooms at this simple bed and breakfast. Not as pretty inside as it is outside, but the rooms have private facilities and there's parking. Check in only between 1130 and 1800.

Podere San Lorenzo, Via Allori 80, Loc Strada, **T** 0588 39080, www.agriturismosanlorenzo.it. *3 km outside Volterra*. Self-catering. Set in peaceful olive groves, this is a farm-based *agriturismo* round a 12th-century monastery, now converted into comfortably rustic apartments and rooms. Breakfast and dinner are available and bookings can be taken for one night as well as a full week. Delightful views, reasonable prices and a natural swimming pool – it's chemical free so gets a bit green, but the frogs love it.

Villa Opera, Monte Volterrano, Loc Villa, **T** 0588 81317, www.villaopera.it. Self-catering. Country house on the edge of Volterra that has nine apartments, sleeping from two to six people. They're clean and attractively furnished, although the kitchens aren't as large or well equipped as you'd wish. A basket of snacks is provided when you arrive and guests have use of a small pool. Possible to book for one night only in low season.

Villa Palagione, east of Volterra, **T** 0588 39014, www.villa-palagione.com. *About 4 km off the SS 439*. Self-catering. Imposing 16th-century villa that was once an aristocratic country seat. Frescoes adorn the rooms and there are lovely formal gardens. It was rescued from ruin in the 1980s and turned into a cultural centre. Both individuals and groups can stay here and activities on offer range from walking and cooking to riding, language classes and alabaster workshops. Meals are also served.

Camping Le Balze, Via di Mandringa 15, **T** 0588-87880. *2 km from Volterra, on northern outskirts of the town, outside the walls*. Basic campsite with pitches for tents and camper vans.

North of Siena: Chianti

L Relais San Felice, Loc San Felice, **T** 0577 3964,
www.borgosanfelice.com. *6 km west of Castelnuovo Berardenga*.
It doesn't come much swisher than this, a whole *borgo* (medieval
hamlet) transformed into a pristine hotel complex. It has its own
chapel, tennis courts, swimming pool, beauty salon, *enoteca* and
restaurants. Perfect for honeymooners.

L Relais Villa Arceno, Loc Arceno, San Gusmè, **T** 0577 359292,
www.relaisvillarceno.com. *North of Castelnuovo Berardenga*.
Secluded 17th-century villa tucked away at the end of a long
drive lined with cypresses. Rooms are elegant and refined,
there's a private chapel, pool and vineyard. The restaurant's
open for non-residents.

AL Castello di Spaltenna, Gaiole in Chianti, **T** 0577 749483,
www.spaltenna.it. Secluded bliss and discreet service in this
medieval castle with swimming pools, sauna, gym and tennis
court. Many rooms have four-poster beds.

A Relais Vignale, Via Pianigiani 8, Radda in Chianti, **T** 0577
738300, www.vignale.it. All the rooms are slightly different in
this de-luxe hotel in the village. Swimming pool, lounges with
comfy chairs and a library for guests.

A Villa Curina Resort, Loc Curina, **T** 0577 355630,
www.villacurina.it. *4.5 km west of Castelnuovo Berardenga*.
Brick and beam ceilings, antique furnishings and contemporary
comforts at this 17th-century villa. As well as a pool there's a
lovely garden complete with pomegranate trees and a terrace
with sweeping views.

B Il Colombaio, Via Chiantigiana, Castellina in Chianti, **T** 0577 740444, www.albergoilcolombaio.it. Old farmhouse on the outskirts of the village, that is now a three-star hotel. Rooms are small but attractively furnished and there's a small swimming pool too.

B Palazzo Squarcialupi, Via Ferruccio 22, Castellina in Chianti, **T** 0577 741186, www.chiantiandrelax.com. *Closed Nov-Mar.* Conveniently placed in the centre of the village, this lovely hotel in a 14th-century palace is furnished with antique pieces. Large terrace for drinks in summer, frescoes on the walls, huge fireplaces and beamed ceilings. They also have an *agriturismo* near the village, with three apartments sleeping from two to four people.

C Podere Terreno, Via della Volpaia, **T** 0577 738312, www.podereterreno.it. *Near Radda in Chianti.* Comfy, rustic atmosphere at this welcoming, 16th-century farmhouse in the country. Dogs snooze on sofas and copper pots hang from the beamed ceiling. Rooms are small, but very clean, with their own facilities and everyone dines together at night – either round the long table in the kitchen or outside on the terrace. Food is very good and fresh, and the wine comes from the family's vineyards. They also offer cooking lessons.

Casa Selvolini, Volpaia, **T/F** 0577 738329. *North of Radda in Chianti.* Self-catering. Two spotless apartments in part of Volpaia's ancient castle, owned by Lina Selvolini's family for 300 years. Glorious views, stone steps and original features like slit windows for shooting arrows.

Castello di Cacchiano, Monti in Chianti, **T** 0577 747018, cacchiano@chianticlassico.com. Self-catering. Eleventh-century castle with large wine-producing estate. It has two, large apartments, well equipped and with plenty of atmosphere. Good for large family groups.

Castello di Fonterutoli, Fonterutoli, booking through Stagioni del Chianti, **T** 055 265 7842, www.stagionidelchianti.com. Self-catering. Charming apartments in pretty medieval village, owned since 1435 by the Mazzei family. The smallest is **Carpentiere**, which sleeps two; the largest, **Limonaia**, sleeps seven. Small, shared swimming pool with views of Siena. Ask Valentina to show you the family's wine cellar – it's an old prison. There are no shops or restaurants in the village, so come prepared.

Le Bonatte, Loc Le Bonatte, Radda in Chianti, **T** 0577 758783, www.lebonatte.it. Self-catering in a converted farmhouse and outbuildings a short distance from the village, with one large house sleeping 10 people and a small apartment sleeping four. Daily rents are available in the small apartment.

Podere San Giuseppe, Strada Val di Sambra 6, Castelnuovo Berardenga, **T** 0577 355436, vetreriavka@libero.it. Self-catering. Striking villa recently converted into three immaculate, roomy and tastefully furnished apartments. Power showers, panoramic views, swimming pool and large terrace. Katy will cook for you if you wish and can organize breakfast. Unusually for self-catering, they'll allow two-night stays.

Residence Catignano, Loc Catignano, **T** 0577 356744, www.villacatignano.it. *5 km northwest of Pianella*. Self-catering. The Sergardi family have lived here for over 400 years and the estate is filled with a relaxed, family atmosphere. Buildings have been beautifully converted into apartments, and cats laze around the classical Italian garden. There are formal and elegant apartments in the 17th-century villa and country-style apartments in the *fattoria* outbuildings. From the swimming pool you can see the towers of distant Siena.

East of Siena

Arezzo

A-B Hotel I Portici, Portici di Via Roma 18, **T** 0575 403132, www.hoteliportici.com. Small and opulent, this hotel makes a statement with leopard-skin prints, chandeliers and colourful drapes. Rooms are all slightly different but comfortable, and some have balconies. Reception is covered with photos of past guests, including Joaquín Cortés and Collina, the famous bald international football referee.

C Hotel Continentale, Piazza Guido Monaco 7, **T** 0575 20251, www.hotelcontentale.com. Lots of floral wallpaper and furnishings in the rooms and not much character, but the hotel's clean and comfortable and has a convenient central location and pleasant staff. Street-side rooms are very noisy.

Casa Pippo, Loc Lignano, **T** 0575 910251, www.casapippo.it. *Near Arezzo*. Self-catering. Immaculate and beautifully furnished, this traditional stone house is set in the countryside just a short drive from Arezzo. It's divided into two apartments that can be linked. Sleeps up to eight, the small apartment's suitable for two. There's a swimming pool and the friendly owners take great care to look after you. Good base for riding and walking. Overnight stays are possible in low season.

Cortona

AL Relais Villa Baldelli, San Pietro a Cegliolo 420, **T** 0575 612406, www.villabaldelli.it. *A short drive northwest of Cortona.* Very plush 18th-century villa, set in its own grounds, with a swimming pool, wine-tasting room and an antique stone fireplace in the lounge. The rooms have lots of drapes and beams, and you can breakfast on the terrace in the summer.

A Villa Marsili, Viale Cesare Battisti 13, Cortona, **T** 0575 605252, www.villamarsili.com. *On the edge of the old city, around 12 mins' walk to the centre.* Restored 17th-century villa that manages to combine elegance and comfort. The cast of *Under the Tuscan Sun* stayed here when filming, and other high-profile guests have included Gwyneth Paltrow. Antiques, Murano glass chandeliers and good-sized rooms, many with views.

C-D Corys Hotel, Loc Torreone 6, **T** 0575 605141, www.corys.it. *Northeast of Cortona.* This small hotel in a quiet hamlet is very close to the home of Frances Mayes, author of *Under the Tuscan Sun*. Rooms are simply furnished and clean, and many have stunning views of the Val di Chiana. You can breakfast out on the terrace in summer and there's a restaurant serving good Tuscan dishes.

Il Trebbio and **I Pagliai**, contact Terretrusche, Vicolo Alfieri 3, **T** 575 605287, www.terretrusche.com. *Dotted around countryside near Cortona.* Self-catering. These very high-quality properties are reasonably priced, spotlessly clean and have been beautifully restored. Il Trebbio is divided into three apartments sleeping from four to six people, or can be rented as a whole. It has a swimming pool and lovely grounds, as well as a tiny chapel. I Pagliai is a converted farm with both apartments and rooms available. Breakfast can be provided on request and there's an old wood-fired pizza oven outside.

Eating and drinking

Many visitors never stray from the cafés and restaurants around the Campo, yet exploration is always well rewarded. Food is taken seriously here and every little street and narrow lane seems to hide a restaurant or *trattoria* serving substantial and delicious dishes. Tuscan cuisine manages to combine simplicity with sophistication. Menus feature lots of meat such as wild boar and pork, but vegetarians can eat extremely well on traditional bean soups, pasta dishes and fresh salads and vegetables. The ancient buildings mean that interiors are usually cosy and cavern-like with stone walls and arches, or rustically elegant with frescoes and beamed ceilings. Siena clings to its traditions and, like many Italian cities, isn't open to outside culinary influences; the few ethnic eateries are Chinese, but you're unlikely to feel the need to search them out. Lunch is usually served between 1200 and 1500, and most places don't open in the evening until 1930. When reading menus, remember to check out the *pane e coperto* (bread and cover charge) and the service charge. These can vary enormously and lead to some unpleasant surprises when settling the bill.

Eating codes

Price

¶¶¶	€	30 and over
¶¶	€	20-29
¶	€	19 and under

Prices refer to an average two-course meal without drinks.

Piazza del Campo and around

Cafés and gelaterie

¶ **Caribia**, Via Rinaldini 13, **T** 0577 280823. *1030-2400, closed early Nov-late Feb. Just off the Campo. Map 2, A6, p236* This *gelateria* has possibly the best ice creams in the city.

¶ **Il Palio**, Piazza del Campo, **T** 0577 282055. *0830-0100. Map 2, A5, p236* People-watching heaven and the most popular of the places to eat on the Campo – in prime position opposite the Palazzo Pubblico. Locals as well as tourists love to sit outside and watch the world go by. Apart from coffee they have good *panini*, light pasta dishes and bowls of fresh salad.

¶ **Key Largo**, Via Rinaldini 17, **T** 0577 236339. *Oct-Mar 0700-2200, Apr-Sep 0700-2400. Map 2, A6, p236* Do as the locals do and pop in for a slug of espresso and a pastry. Best is the secret balcony reached by a narrow stairway on the upper floor; the views of the Campo are superb and you'll achieve a sense of superiority over the tourists below who wonder how on earth you got there.

!
● For a description of Tuscan cuisine and wine, see 'A poor man's feast', p217.

¶ **La Costarelli**, Via di Città 33. *0800-2400, closed in winter.*
Map 2, B4, p236 Popular *gelateria* and café. Go to the back
and upstairs to slurp your ice while sitting on their tiny terrace
overlooking the Campo.

Picnic supplies

Mercata della Frutta, Via di Salicotto 31. *Map 2, B6, p236*
If you're self-catering or want some picnic supplies, join the local
ladies squeezing the tomatoes at this greengrocer's near the
Campo. All sorts of vegetables, good-quality fruit and seasonal
produce like fresh *porcini* mushrooms.

Terzo di San Martino

Restaurants

¶¶¶ **Cane & Gatto**, Via Pagliaresi 6, **T** 0577 333879. *Fri-Wed
2000-2200, sometimes opens for lunch. Map 2, D10, p237* Small,
with contemporary prints, glass tables and the odd antique, this
one's for serious gourmets. Run by a friendly married couple, it has
a 'tasting menu' (€61) of around six dishes, made with the best
local and seasonal produce they can find, as well as a fine selection
of wines. You'll need to book and they're happy to cater for
veggies with advance warning.

¶¶¶ **Le Logge**, Via del Porrione 31, **T** 0577 48013. *Mon-Sat
1200-1500, 1900-2300. Map 2, B6, p236* Doors open onto the street
revealing old prints, antiques, walls lined with bottles of wine and
the buzz of serious diners. It's one of the best-known places in the
city serving lots of local meat like lamb and beef in sophisticated
sauces. The wide selection of wines includes a distinctive *Brunello di
Montalcino*. The sort of place where you'll want to dress up.

Nello, Via del Porrione 28, **T** 0577 289043. *Mon-Sat 1200-1500, 1900-2200*. *Map 2, B6, p236* The contemporary black tables and metal seats make a welcome antidote to the ubiquitous 'rustic Tuscan' look. The food's imaginative too, with local produce like wild boar given a fresh treatment. Veggies have an excellent choice: chickpea and artichoke pie, *faggotini* with cheese in saffron sauce, and goats' cheese and aubergine risotto with courgette flowers. Watch the 13% service charge.

La Finestra, Piazza del Mercato 14, **T** 0577 42093. *Mon-Sat 1200-1500, 1900-2200 and Sun evening*. *Map 2, C6, p236* The outside seats look over the marketplace and the back of Palazzo Pubblico, inside it's fresh and airy with pink and green checked tablecloths and straw-bottom chairs. Daily specials chalked on the board outside and lots of Sienese and Tuscan produce to try like *ribollita*, *pici* and wild boar. Veggies can go for dishes like *tagliatelle* with rocket and rosemary.

Trattorie, osterie and pizzerie

Fori Porta, Via C Tolomei 1, **T** 0577 222100. *Tue-Sun 1230-1430, 1930-2300*. *About 5 mins' walk outside the Porta Romana*. *Map 3, L8, p237* Authentic neighbourhood *trattoria*. Not many tourists make it here, but it offers dishes like steak with rosemary for €12, or *fagottini al dragoncello* (pasta with tarragon) €7. Leave room for some fig and walnut tart, or their speciality, a delicious chocolate cake. You can walk it off on the way back.

da Gano, Via di Pantaneto 146, **T** 0577 22194. *Wed-Mon 1200-1430, 1900-2230*. *Map 2, B8, p237* Relax with the locals down in the student district: cheery blue checked tablecloths and lots of pictures of past Palios on the walls. It's a good place to try Tuscan dishes like *tortelli maremmani* (handmade filled pasta from the Maremma) or a local favourite, *trippa alla Senese* – that's tripe to you.

Osteria del Coro, Via di Pantaneto 85, **T** 0577 222482 *Lunch and dinner. Map 2, B8, p237* Dark and cosy, with lots of prints and wine bottles dotted about and a comfortable bustle. Travellers on shoestrings love the pizzas from €4, while those feeling more flush can go for the local cheeses, meats and good range of wines. Dishes are filling like potato and *porcini* pie, or *tagliatelle* with pork and grapes.

Carla e Franca, Via di Pantaneto 6, **T** 0577 284385. *1100-1500, 1700-2300. Map 2, C10, p237* Simple pizzeria that also does takeaways. Brown paper place mats, tumblers, no frills. Pizzas are thin, crispy and freshly made and there are over 40 types to choose from.

Il Papei, Piazza del Mercato 6, **T** 0577 280894. *Tue-Sun 1200-1500, 1900-2230. Map 2, C6, p236* Cheery *trattoria*, down in the rather unlikely surroundings of the marketplace, with plenty of tables squeezed onto the pavement outside. Green checked cloths and red bent-back chairs make for laid-back dining. Dishes might include *pappardelle* with wild-boar sauce, or breasts of chicken.

! Italy is now officially smoke free and it's an offence to smoke in bars, restaurants and cafés. Whether the locals will adhere to the new ruling is another matter.

Terzo di Città

Restaurants

¶¶¶ Al Marsili, Via del Castoro 3, **T** 0577 47154. *Tue-Sun 1230-1500, 1930-2300. Map 2, D4, p236* Serious dining under the arched brick ceilings of the Palazzo Marsili's cellar, with some secluded alcoves for those craving privacy. The menu features meat like *cinghiale* (wild boar) or *faraona* (guinea fowl), the latter cooked with prunes, pine nuts and almonds. The set lunch for €22 is popular with locals and you'll see whole families eating here for Sunday lunch.

¶¶¶ Antica Osteria da Divo, Via Franciosa 29, **T** 0577 284381. *Wed-Mon 1200-1430, 1900-2200. Map 2, B1, p236* Troglodyte dining in atmospheric cellars, with crisp white cloths on the tables, and fine gold-rimmed china. Cuisine is creative Tuscan and reflects the seasons. You might find risotto with green tomatoes in *pecorino*, or main courses like duck in *vin santo* with herb tart, or beef and bacon in courgette flowers with potato pie.

¶¶¶ San Desiderio, Vicolo delle Campane 2, **T** 0577 286091. *Wed-Mon 1200-1430, 1930-2230. Map 2, B4, p236* Squeezed down behind the Duomo, this restaurant offers a set menu for €30. You can find starters like *pecorino* drizzled with honey, followed by steak, or pasta with truffles if in season.

Trattorie, osterie and pizzerie

¶¶ Castelvecchio, Via Castelvecchio 85, **T** 0577 49586. *Mon-Sat 1230-1430, 1930-2130. Map 2, F4, p236* Rather like a cavern, with exposed brick ceiling and tiled floors, this cosy *osteria* serves dishes like *risotto con cipolline al vin santo* (chives and local wine) for

€9.50. There's a tasting menu of four courses for €25 (minimum two people).

¶ **Il Dinaio dell'Eremita**, Via delle Cerchia 2, **T** 0577 49490. *Mon-Sat. Map 2, G4, p236* There's a suitably intimate, rustic feel to this tiny *osteria* down in the Contrada della Tartuca (Turtle). They specialize in ancient Sienese cuisine. You can start with hearty *crostone* slathered with *porcini* or ricotta and spinach, try spelt soup, various cured meats or strong *pecorino* cheese.

¶¶ **Taverna di San Giuseppe**, Via Giovanni Duprè 132, **T** 0577 42286. *Mon-Sat 1215-1445, 1915-2145. Map 2, F5, p236* There's an intimate feel to dining under the brick arches of this traditional taverna. Lots of Tuscan dishes to choose from including *trippa senese*, *gnocchi verdi* with herbs, and chicken with *porcini* mushrooms.

¶ **University Canteen**, Via Sant' Agata. *Mon-Sat 1230-1500, 1930-2130. Map 2, F5, p236* Students can take advantage of this great-value canteen that does a slick line in self-service sandwiches, salads and hearty plates of pasta to sustain students through gruelling hours. Just 80 cents for coffee, €3 for *panini*. Get there early otherwise it's pretty chaotic.

Cafés

¶ **Fiorella**, Via di Città 13, **T** 0577 271255, 0700-1930. *Mon-Sat. Map 2, B4, p236* If you want a quick slug of coffee or a snack, this friendly little café/bar does the job. It's a bit of a squeeze to find room at the wooden counter sometimes, but that's part of the charm.

Enoteca

Cantina in Piazza, Via Casato di Sotto 24, **T** 0577 222758. *Mon-Sat. Map 2, C5, p236* Come at around 1900 for aperitifs and feast on a great selection of local meats, cheeses and salads. You pay for a glass of wine – €3.50 for Chianti, €8 for Brunello – and you can eat as much as you want. Sandwiches and some local cakes at lunchtime.

Enoteca Sant'Agata, Via Sant'Agata 8. *Tue-Thu 1000-2000, Mon, Wed and Fri 1700-2000, Sat and Sun 1000-1400, 1600-2000. Map 2, F4, p236* Tiny *enoteca* in the Contrada dell'Onda (Wave) where you can try Tuscan wines by the glass: €3 for Chianti, up to €6 for Brunello. Lots of other Tuscan foods to take home, including the famous *lardo di Colonnata* (see p218).

Picnic supplies

La Bottega, Via di Città 154. *Mon-Sat 0730-2000. Map 2, D3, p236* This general store is a convenient place to get picnic supplies. There are cheeses, olives, lots of different salamis and bread. It's a short stop from the Campo and is next to a fruit shop, so you can get everything at once.

Le Campane, Vicolo delle Campane 9, **T** 0577 282290. *Mon, Tue and Thu-Sat 0800-1315, 1700-2000, Sun 0800-1315. Map 2, C4, p236* Lovely cakes and fresh pastries.

Eating and drinking

Terzo di Camollia

Restaurants

¶¶¶ Tre Cristi, Vicolo di Provenzano 1/7, **T** 0577 280608.
1230-1430, 1930-2230. Map 3, D11, p239 You can peer into the
bustling kitchen from the street. This is serious dining, with crisp
white cloths and candles on the tables, and *contrade* symbols
on the walls. Cuisine is Mediterranean with a contemporary twist,
so look out for antipasti like octopus with chickpeas on *pecorino*
cheese and *primi* like champagne risotto with mullet and pumpkin
flowers. They do a six-course gourmet menu for €50. Best to book.

¶¶¶-¶¶ La Buca di Porsenna, Via delle Donzelle 1, **T** 0577 44431.
Wed-Mon 1230-1430, 1930-2300. Map 3, G10, p239 Established
central restaurant. Try the *pici* – Sienese thick spaghetti – with a
meat sauce, or *ribollita* – soup made with bread and vegetables.

¶¶¶-¶¶ Il Biondo, Via del Rustichetto, **T** 0577 280739. *Thu-Tue
1200-1430, 1900-2215. Map 3, D8, p239* The outdoor seating area
may say 'tourist' but locals make their way here as well, attracted
by specialities like *pici ai porcini* (€9 if in season) or Sienese cutlets.
There's food from all over Italy, with huge slabs of *polenta*, risottos
and gnocchi on the menu too.

¶¶ Enzo, Via Camollia 49, **T** 0577 281277. *Mon-Sat 1200-1430,
2000-2230. Map 3, A6, p238* Slightly off the beaten track but
worth seeking out, both for serious foodies and romantics.
Large photos of old Siena, white linen, and pleasant staff serving
imaginative dishes such as *pecorino* flan or gnocchi with black
cabbage and parmesan. They do a five-course Tuscan set menu
(€28), as well as meat and fish tasting menus (veggies catered
for especially with advance warning). Wonderfully calorific

desserts like apple cake with *vin santo*, *ricciarelli* with amaretto sauce or chocolate and vanilla rice pudding.

♯♯ Il Sasso, Via dei Rossi 2, **T** 0577 247049. *Mon-Sat 1215-1445, 1900-2200. Map 3, D10, p239* A bit touristy but conveniently situated off the main shopping street on the way down to San Francesco church. Come for local dishes like *pici* with parmesan and black pepper or Tuscan roast rabbit.

Trattorie, osterie and pizzerie

♯ La Chiacchera, Costa di Sant'Antonio 4, **T** 0577 280631. *Wed-Mon 1200-1530, 1900-2400. Map 3, F7, p239* Excellent value (no cover charge) and rustic Tuscan food. The menu's written on a scrap of paper and they don't serve fripperies like coffee, but you can try good *penne al pomodoro* for €4, traditional sausage and beans, and hearty casseroles. Be prepared to share a table; if you're outside the waiter sticks a wooden block under your seat to stop it wobbling on the steep hill. Best to reserve.

♯ Il Grattacielo, Via dei Pontani 8, **T** 0577 289326. *Mon-Sat 0800-1500, 1730-2000. Map 3, E9, p239* Ironically called 'the skyscraper' due to its low ceiling, this tiny *osteria* practically bulges with local workers at lunchtime. The owners serve the best they can find each day and dish out heaps of potatoes, beans, slices of *proscuitto* and olives from behind the counter. It's cheery, chaotic and great value: an authentic slice of old Siena.

♯ di Nonno Mede, Camporegio 21, **T** 0577 247966. *1230-1500, 1930-2400. Map 3, F6, p238* Tucked down behind San Domenico church, this place is worth coming to just for the view of the Duomo from the seats outside. They offer a very wide choice of pizzas from around €5, covered with everything from artichokes to seafood. White pizzas (no layer of tomato sauce) also feature with simple toppings like oil and rosemary. Good choice of waistband-busting puds.

Cafés and gelaterie

⫟ Bar Monte, Via Banchi di Sopra 95-99, **T** 0577 281094. *Bar 0740-2040, gelateria summer 1100-2400, winter 1100-2000. Map 3, E9, p239* A turn-of-the-last-century look in this little café/bar/*gelateria* with dark wood and lots of mirrors. Pop in for coffee, a cone or a little cake.

⫟ Giusti Continentali, Via dei Rossi 107, **T** 0577 236640. *0730-2000. Map 3, D10, p239* If you're suffering for want of a good cup of tea, this sleek little shop has over 80 to choose from. They've got three rather twee tables at the back and also serve satiny hot chocolate. Remember to crook your little finger when you raise your cup.

⫟ Nannini, Via Banchi di Sopra 24, **T** 0577 236009. *Mon-Sat 0730-2300, Sun 0800-2100 (2000 in winter). Map 3, E9, p239* A Sienese institution, though locals claim it's not what it was. Owned by a family that includes a former Formula One star and a rock singer, this is where people come for pre-work cappuccino or a shot of espresso to sustain them while shopping. There are seats at the back, but to fit in, simply prop up the counter while trying some *ricciarelli* or tooth-cracking, aniseed-laced *cavallucci*.

Picnic supplies

⫟ Forno dei Galli, 45 Via dei Termini, **T** 0577 289073. *Mon-Sat 0730-2000. Map 3, F9, p239* Good bakery (Sclavi chain) serving slices of pizza for lunch on the run, as well as fresh bread, rolls, homemade *ricciarelli* and *panforte*.

★ Best

Cafés

- Nannini, Siena, p134
- Fiaschetteria Italiana, Montalcino, p138
- L'Incontro, Volterra, p143
- Caffè dei Costanti, Arezzo, p149
- Tuscher, Cortona, p152

South of Siena

Montepulciano

ΨΨΨ-ΨΨ **La Grotta**, Via di San Biagio, **T** 0578 757479. *Mar-Dec Thu-Tue 1230-1415, 1930-2200. Opposite San Biagio church on the edge of town.* It looks fairly modest from the outside but this restaurant, beautifully situated opposite San Biagio church, has a deserved reputation for the best food in town. Taglionini pasta might be mixed with artichokes and bacon, and steaks are tender. There's a tasting menu for €42 for those who want a bit of everything.

ΨΨ **Le Logge del Vignola**, Via delle Erbe 6, **T** 0578 717290. *Wed-Mon 1230-1430, 1930-2230.* Wooden floors, a beamed ceiling and tasty Tuscan dishes that attract locals as well as visitors. Imaginative touches – loin of rabbit might be served with fresh figs and balsamic vinegar – and there's a good selection of local cheese.

Ψ **Osteria Acquacheta**, Via del Teatro 22, **T** 0578 758443. *Wed-Mon 1230-1500, 1930-2230.* This simple but popular little place by the grand Teatro Poliziano offers Tuscan favourites like Sienese *pici*, as well as a tasty plate of *pecorino*. Best to book.

Trattoria di Cagnano, Via dell'Opio nel Corso 30,
T 0578 758757. *Tue-Sun 1230-1430, 1930-2230*. Relaxed *trattoria*
that does very tasty pizzas, made in their wood-fired oven. As well
as all the usual favourites, they offer ones topped with *lardo di
Colonnata* or (when in season) fresh *porcini*.

Caffè Poliziano, Via di Voltaia nel Corso 27, **T** 0578 758615.
0700-2400. There's a lovely sepia tinge to this historic café, which
retains its Liberty-style interior with parlour palms, a piano, and
walls lined with mirrors and prints. On fine days there's a tussle to
get the seats on the little terrace, which has glorious views of the
Chiana valley – you can even see Lago Trasimeno in Umbria.

Pienza

Dal Falco, Piazza Dante Alighieri 3, **T** 0578 748551. *Sat-Thu
for lunch and dinner*. Just on the edge of the town, this restaurant
serves good homemade pasta, and main dishes such as traditional
Florentine steaks. It's unpretentious and good value.

La Buca delle Fate, Corso Il Rossellino 38, **T** 0578 748448.
Tue-Sun 1230-1400, 1900-2130. Among Pienza's many eateries
is this large, airy *trattoria* with an arched ceiling and red-tiled
floor. It offers traditional Tuscan dishes like *pici* and gets busy
at weekends.

Il Caffè, Piazza Dante Alighieri 10, **T** 0578 748718. *Daily*.
Friendly little café serving locals with slugs of espresso,
cakes and sandwiches.

Places to eat an ice cream

- Sitting on Il Campo, Siena, p31
- In the botanical gardens, Siena, p52
- From the walls of Pienza, p66
- The square in San Gimignano, p78
- The balcony at La Costarelli, Siena, p126

Montalcino

🍴 **Trattoria Sciame**, Via Ricasoli 9, **T** 0577 848017. *Wed-Mon 1200-1430, 1900-2130*. Cheaper and less touristy than many other eateries in the town, this *trattoria* has pink tablecloths, green wooden chairs and a beamed ceiling. The food's excellent. Dishes might include *tagliatelle* with truffle sauce, beef cooked in the local Brunello wine, pork with rosemary or ravioli with butter and sage.

🍴 **Il Grappolo Blu**, Scale di Via Moglio 1, **T** 0577 847150. *Sat-Thu for lunch and dinner*. Unpretentious *trattoria* where you can get authentic Tuscan dishes. Look out for *pici* with garlic and cherry tomatoes, or onions cooked in balsamic vinegar. Meats like rabbit are often cooked in Brunello. Good idea to reserve.

🍴 **Enoteca La Fortezza**, Piazzale Fortezza, **T** 0577 849211. *Apr-Oct daily 0900-2000, Nov-Mar Mon-Sat 0900-1800*. Atmospherically situated in the old fortress this is a great place to taste the local wines and olive oils, as well as snack on bruschetta, salami or *pecorino* cheese. Around 130 different types of Brunello to buy, as well as lots of other Italian wine – they'll ship it home for you. If you just want a glass of Brunello it'll cost €10.

Eating and drinking

¶ Fiaschetteria Italiana, Piazza del Popolo 6, **T** 0577 849043. *Summer daily 0730-2400, closed Thu in winter*. Historic café that dates back to 1888 and retains a period atmosphere. Striking Liberty-style interior with large mirrors, velvet sofas and local people enjoying a glass of the famous Brunello or a quick espresso.

San Quirico d'Orcia and around

¶¶ Il Tinaio, Via Dante Alighieri 35a, San Quirico d'Orcia, **T** 0577 898347. *Fri-Wed 1100-1900*. In summer you can eat outside at this restaurant, which serves primi like *ribollita* and main courses such as *faraona* (guinea fowl) in *vin santo*. No credit cards under €26.

¶¶ Ristorante del Castello, Piazza Vittorio Emanuele II, San Giovanni d'Asso, **T** 0577 802939. *Thu-Tue 1230-1430, 1930-2200*. Popular spot for a bite, as it has seats outside and during the truffle season it's a good place to taste the local delicacy. Dishes might include ravioli with butter, sage and truffles; wild boar with polenta or beef in red wine.

¶¶ Trattoria al Vecchio Forno, Via Piazzola 8, San Quirico d'Orcia, **T** 0577 897380. *Thu-Tue 1200-1500, 1900-2200*. Good-value tasty food with a menu that might feature omelette with *pecorino*, chicken in Brunello or baked ricotta and kale dumplings.

¶ Eraldo's, Lucignano d'Asso, outside San Quirico d'Orcia, **T** 0577 803109. *Tue-Sun 0800-2000*. Eraldo's the old gentleman who runs this charming traditional shop/café/restaurant. Ask anyone in this tiny village and they'll tell you where it is. Pop in to buy cheeses, wines and fruit for a picnic; have a quick coffee or enjoy a meal in the evening. Book before 1930 to eat at night.

¶ La Bottega delle Crete, Via XX Settembre 22, San Giovanni d'Asso, **T** 0577 803076. *Tue-Sun 1200-2000.* Shop/*osteria* where you can find all sorts of local cold cuts and cheeses and white truffles in season.

¶ La Torre, Monte Oliveto Maggiore, **T** 0577 707022. *Wed-Mon 1200-1500, 1900-2200; bar 0900-2400.* Picturesque medieval tower conveniently situated by the abbey of Monte Oliveto Maggiore. Open for snacks, coffees or more substantial dishes like lasagne.

¶ Taverna di Ciacco, Via Dante Alighieri 30a, San Quirico d'Orcia, **T** 0577 897312. *Wed-Mon 0730-2400.* Pleasant, relaxed atmosphere at this café/wine bar on the main square. Serves sandwiches, *crostini* and snacks.

West of Siena

Colle di Val d'Elsa and around

¶¶¶ Arnolfo, Via XX Settembre 50, Colle di Val d'Elsa, **T** 0577 920549. *Thu-Mon lunch and dinner.* New-wave Tuscan cookery and panoramic views in this restaurant run by two brothers. The menu changes frequently and might feature Crete Senesi goat with apples, or beef from the Chianina valley. There's a comprehensive, but pricey, wine list.

¶¶¶ La Scuderia di Mensano, Via Ricasoli 25, Loc Mensano, Casole d'Elsa, **T** 0577 963911. *Fri-Wed 1230-1400, 1930-2100. About 12 km southwest of Colle di Val d'Elsa.* In a picturesque hamlet, this is a fine dining restaurant, situated in a former stable block. Vegetarians are well catered for with dishes like home-made nettle gnocchi with dolcelatte sauce or gorgonzola soufflé with caramelized walnuts and poached pears. Main courses might include herb-crusted lamb fillet with vegetables. Save room for gorgeous puds like chocolate tart and green fig ice cream. It's the place to come for a special occasion. They run cookery courses on Thursdays.

Dietro le Quinte, Vicolo della Misericordia 14, Colle di Val d'Elsa, **T** 0577 920458. *1200-1430, 1900-2230*. Lovely views over the surrounding countryside from the terrace of this restaurant tucked behind the theatre. Main courses include a seafood risotto, and there's also a 'tasting menu' at €35.

L'Angolo di Sapia, Bastione di Sapia, Colle di Val d'Elsa. *1200-1500, 1900-2400*. Restaurant with outside terrace, worth considering for a cheap meal or a drink.

Nencini Piero, Piazza Arnolfo di Cambio 4, Colle di Val d'Elsa, **T** 0577 920082, *Thu-Tue, all day*. Pleasant café in main square in the lower part of town. Good cakes.

Il Pozzo, Piazza Roma 20, Monteriggioni, **T** 0577 304127, *1215-1445, 1945-2200, closed Sun evening and Mon. About 10 km southeast of Colle di Val d'Elsa*. Highly rated Tuscan food in the centre of the old fortress town of Monteriggioni.

San Gimignano

Ristorante Dorandò, Vicolo dell'Oro 2, **T** 0577 941 862. *Summer daily 1230-1430, 1930-2130, winter Tue-Sun*. Reservations are essential, even for lunch, at this sophisticated restaurant. It's a place to linger over dishes inspired by ancient Tuscan recipes: look for *pici* pasta laced with mint and walnuts, *tagliatelle* with pumpkin and truffles, or rabbit with spices. Extensive list of Tuscan wines, including those by little-known producers.

** Dulcis in Fundo**, Via degli Innocenti 21, **T** 0577 941919. *Thu-Tue 1230-1500, 1930-2145*. On a quiet street that looks over the countryside, this restaurant serves Tuscan dishes with a modern twist. You might find *cinta senese*, the local pork, with roast potatoes or meat served with blue cheese, walnuts and honey. Desserts range from traditional *cantucci* with *vin santo*, to a cake made with pumpkin, vanilla, chocolate and saffron.

- Osteria del Carcere, Via del Castello 13, **T** 0577 941905. *Fri-Tue open for lunch and dinner, Thu dinner only*. Just off the main square this *osteria* is popular with locals seeking some good salamis and hot Tuscan dishes. They also do delicious desserts and have a good selection of wines.

** Caffè Erbe**, Via Diacceto 1, **T** 0577 907083. *Summer 0830-2400, winter 0830-2000*. Pleasant, contemporary café behind the Duomo serving *panini*, coffees and snacks. They've got an internet connection and also do wine tastings.

** Chiribiri**, Piazzetta della Madonna 1, **T** 0577 941948. *1100-2300*. You could easily miss this excellent trattoria, as it's tucked away in a side street near Porta San Giovanni. Landscape prints on the walls, white cloths on the tables and great-value traditional food. The menu changes all the time, but might include *ossobuco*, *tagliatelle* with *fungi porcini* – and apple tart for pudding.

** La Cisterna**, Piazza delle Cisterna, **T** 0577 940423. *Open most days till late*. Okay, the seats outside this café are crammed with tourists, but sitting here is a lovely way to soak up San Gimignano's distinctive charms.

¶ La Mandragola, Via Berignano 58, **T** 0577 940377. *Mar-Oct daily 1200-1430, 1900-2200, Nov-Feb Fri-Wed*. Spacious restaurant serving reasonably priced Tuscan dishes. Look for things like *pappardelle* with wild boar sauce, duck in *vin santo* or wild boar in Chianti.

Gelaterie Two *gelaterie* battle it out on Piazza della Cisterna. Most famous is **Gelateria di Piazza**, at No 4, which is in all the guides – and was Tony Blair's choice. Less celebrated, but preferred by many locals, are the ices at **Caffetteria dell'Olmo** at No 34. You can always try both, of course.

Volterra and around

¶¶¶-¶¶ Da Bado, Borgo San Lazzero 9, Volterra, **T** 0588 86477. *Thu-Tue 1230-1400, 1900-2130, bar 0700-2200*. One of the few places serving traditional Volterran dishes. *Primi* might include *pappa al pomodoro* (a tomato and bread stew), *zuppa alla volterrana* (bread, bean and vegetable stew), home-made *pasta alla chitarra* (square spaghetti) with anchovy and shallot sauce. Meaty mains include meats like pigeon, Volterran-style tripe stewed in a tomato and herb sauce, or salted cod stewed with onions. Reservations recommended.

¶¶ Albana, Mazzolla village, **T** 0588 39001. *Wed-Mon 1230-1400, 1900-2130. Approx 10 km from Volterra on SS68*. Locals and visitors flock to this small restaurant in sleepy Mazzolla, housed in a converted stable. Anna, the chef, produces seasonal antipasti and delicious home-made pasta, such as barley-stuffed ravioli with a butter and balsamic vinegar sauce, *papardelle* with game ragout, or pumpkin *tortellini* stuffed with ricotta and pinenuts. Lots of game for mains, tasty fresh desserts, and good house wine, served in traditional Tuscan hay-wrapped bottles. Reservations recommended.

❝❞ Etruria, Piazza dei Priori 6-8, Volterra, **T** 0588 86064. *Thu-Tue lunch and dinner.* Ornately decorated walls and ceilings make this one of the prettiest restaurants to visit. There's a tourist menu and dishes might include *pappardelle* with hare sauce.

❝❞ La Grotta, Via Turazza 13, Volterra, **T** 0588 85336. *Thu-Tue 1230-1500, 1930-2200.* Friendly little restaurant with cheerful yellow tablecloths and tables outside in summer. Start with a plate of *pecorino* cheese with acacia honey, then try imaginative dishes such as sausage and balsamic vinegar risotto, or chickpea crêpes with *porcini* mushrooms.

❝❞ Sacco Fiorentino, Piazza XX Settembre, Volterra, **T** 0588 88537. *1200-1445, 1900-2145.* Refined, innovative dishes based on seasonal ingredients, and daily seafood specialities. Desserts are good too and there's a comprehensive wine list.

❝ Antica Osteria Roncolla, **T** 0588 39111. *Apr-Oct 1200-2300, closed Thu. 2 km outside Volterra on SS68 towards Siena.* Informal eaterie by the roadside, that only has outdoor seating – so weather dependent. Lovely views and a long menu that mixes Tuscan and Sardinian traditions. Simple sandwiches, hot meals and home-made desserts. Try the *pane curacau*, a crisp Sardinian bread that's stuffed and then heated. Often live music in summer.

❝ L'Antica Taverna, Via dei Sarti 18-22, Volterra, **T** 0588 87058. *Thu-Tue 1200-1500, 1900-2100 (approx).* High brick walls and original beams at this simple taverna. Pizzas start at €4.20 and mains at €7.50.

❝ L'Incontro, Via Matteotti 18, Volterra **T** 0588 80500. *Daily till late.* Marble-topped tables and walls lined with wine bottles at this busy café/bar that's also an *enoteca*. Join local people for a bowl of Volterrana soup that's served on a slice of bread, cold cuts or delicious cakes. In summer they serve ice creams too, in winter chocolates.

¶ **La Tavernetta**, Via Guarnacci 14, Volterra, **T** 0588 87630. *Wed-Mon 1200-1530, 1830-2230*. Baroque frescoes embellish the ceiling at this popular pizzeria. Pizzas to take away as well.

¶ **La Vena di Vino**, Via Don Minzoni 30, Volterra, **T** 0588 81491. *Wed-Mon 0930-late*. Lovely, cosy little *enoteca* run by Bruno and Lucio, who also serve simple, good-quality food. Best for things like cold cuts and cheese, you might get delicious beans with a bowl of melted cheese, *pecorino* with drizzles of honey, or local meats. Good choice of wine too.

¶ **Ombra della Sera**, Via Guarnacci 16, Volterra, **T** 0588 85274. *Tue-Sun 1200-1500, 1900-2200*. Red seats, tiled floors and a wide selection of pizzas at reasonable prices. If you want a change from the usual *margherita* try a *maremmana* – it's topped with wild boar.

Enoteca Scali, Via Guarnacci 3, Volterra, **T** 0588 81170. *Summer Tue-Sun, winter Tue-Sat 0900-1300, 1600-2000*. Good choice of wines, local cheeses, cold cuts and cakes for picnics.

La Mangia Toia, Via Gramsci, Volterra. *Thu-Tue*. Cheap and tasty slices of pizza and kebabs to take away.

North of Siena: Chianti

¶¶¶ **Al Gallopapa**, Via delle Volte 14, Castellina in Chianti, **T** 0577 742939. *Wed-Sun 1930-2130*. Squeezed under the arches that ring the village, this well-known restaurant is a bit like a medieval cavern. Over 400 wines to choose from and a pricey menu.

¶¶¶ Da Antonio, Via Fiorita 38, Castelnuovo Berardenga, **T** 0577 355321. *Tue-Sun 1230-1430, 1930-2230.* Acclaimed fish restaurant, with a menu featuring the freshest produce available. You might find spaghetti with clams, octopus or sea bass – it depends what's the best.

¶¶¶ La Bottega del 30, Via Santa Caterina 2, Castelnuovo Berardenga, **T** 0577 359226. *Sun lunch and dinner, Thu-Mon dinner only.* Think upmarket rustic and you'll get the picture. The food's Tuscan with French influences and the menu might include ravioli with artichokes, or lamb with parmesan. There's a multi-course tasting menu for €54.

¶¶¶ Ristorante della Pieve, Castello di Spaltenna, Gaiole in Chianti, **T** 0577 749483. *Mid Mar-Dec 1300-1430, 2000-2130.* Sophisticated dining in this hotel restaurant situated in the countryside. Once the refectory of a monastery, it has a coffered ceiling and ornate tapestries and paintings on the walls. Ideal for candlelit dinners in a hushed atmosphere. Best to book – and bring your credit card.

¶¶ Il Fondaccio, Via Ferrucio 27, Castellina in Chianti, **T** 0577 741084. *1900-2100.* Cosy pizzeria with knick-knacks and wine bottles dotted around, flickering candles and a wood-fired oven. Over 30 types of pizza to choose from and seats outside in summer.

¶¶ La Bottega, Piazza della Torre 2, Volpaia, **T** 0577 738001. *Mid Mar-Jan Wed-Mon 1200-1500, 1900-1930.* Carla produces wonderful food using vegetables from her father's garden and other local produce. Try the handmade ravioli, a bowl of *ribollita*, or rabbit with *porcini*. Leave room for her mother Gina's speciality dessert, a light chocolate cake. Cookery courses available.

♦♦♦ La Torre, Piazza del Commune, Castellina in Chianti, **T** 0577 740236. *Sat-Thu 1200-1430, 1930-2130*. The Stiaccini family have run this *trattoria* since 1920. Popular with locals, it has exuberant paintings on the ceiling, and walls hung with sepia photos of old Tuscany. Steaks are a speciality, but you can also try traditional tripe, local *cinta senese* pork, home-made pasta and lovely fresh desserts. Large selection of Chianti wines.

♦♦♦ Taverna Vignale, Via Pianigiani 7, Radda in Chianti, **T** 0577 738701. *Thu-Tue 1300-1430, 1930-2130*. Traditional food at this hotel taverna. In summer you can eat outside on the terrace, in winter there's a cosy log fire.

♦♦-♦ Bengadi, Via della Società Operaia 11, Castelnuovo Berardenga, **T** 0577 355116. Tue-Sun 1100-2400. A good choice of wines and traditional dishes like *papardelle al sugo*, and *ossobucco all'senese*. Reasonable prices and relaxed atmosphere. Wine tastings too.

♦ Bar Sandy, Via XI Febbraio 2, Radda in Chianti, **T** 0577 738711. *Tue-Sun 0700-2200*. They make their own ice cream here from March to October, as well as delicious pastries, sandwiches and *panforte*. Good for a quick coffee and a chance to meet the locals.

♦ Bar Ucci, Piazza della Torre 9, Volpaia, **T** 0577 738042. *Tue-Sun 0800-2100*. This wine, like La Bottega (above), is owned by Carla's family; it serves drinks and snacks.

♦ Il Borgo, San Piero in Barca, near Castelnuovo Berardenga, **T** 0577 363029. *Daily*. There's a real neighbourhood feel to this friendly little shop/*enoteca*/restaurant. The menu changes daily, the food's home-made and the produce is local. Worth seeking out.

❢ Il Cantucco, Via Ferrucio, Castellina in Chianti. *Wed-Sun 1730-0100, also Sat 1100-1430*. Café/wine bar in cellar-like setting, with stone walls and ceilings and paintings lining the walls.

❢ Il Carlino d'Oro, Loc San Regolo 33, Gaiole in Chianti, **T** 0577 747136. *Tue-Sun 1230-1430, 1900-2100*. Friendly family *trattoria*, with cheery blue and white checked tablecloths and large windows overlooking the countryside. Snack on *crostini* or *pecorino*, or have a juicy steak or plate of pasta.

❢ Ristorante Semplici, Via Roma 18, Radda in Chianti, **T** 0577 738010. *Thu-Tue lunch only*. No menu, just whatever's cooking that day at this no frills, family eaterie. Good sliced meats, beans and *pasta forno* – a typical pasta stuffed with cheese. Very good value and a favourite with locals.

❢ Tre Porte, Via Trento e Trieste 4-8, Castellina in Chianti, **T** 0577 741163. *Wed-Mon 1215-1510, 1915-2250*. Beamed ceilings, green tablecloths, Tuscan dishes and a good selection of pizzas – which for some reason are only available in the evenings.

Casa Porciatti, Piazza IV Novembre, Radda in Chianti, **T** 0577 738055. *Apr-Oct daily 0800-1300, 1600-2000, Nov-Mar Mon-Sat*. Celebrated grocery shop bursting with dozens of local meats, over 50 types of cheese, wines, honeys, chocolate and loads of other goodies. Great picnic supplies; they'll ship items home if you can't carry everything.

East of Siena

Arezzo

⑪ Buca di San Francesco, Via San Francesco 1, **T** 0575 23271. *Wed-Sun 1200-1430, 1900-2130, Mon 1200-1430, closed 2 weeks in Jul*. Atmospheric medieval feel in this well-established cellar restaurant. Typical Tuscan fare including thick *ribollita*, home-made pasta and the local Chianina beef.

⑪ La Curia, Via di Pescaja 6, **T** 0575 333007. *Fri-Tue 1230-1430, 1930-2200, Thu 1930-2200 only*. Formal, refined restaurant with deep gold walls, gilded chairs, fine china and champagne-coloured tablecloths. Dine in a hushed atmosphere on dishes like *pecorino* fondue with truffles, *porcini* risotto, and large steaks.

⑪ La Lancia d'Oro, Piazza Grande 18, **T** 0575 21033. *Tue-Sat 1230-1530, 1930-2230, Sun 1230-1530*. The green and white regency stripes on the walls of this upmarket restaurant give it the look of a posh marquee. There are crisp tablecloths and cabinets groaning with bottles of wine. The menu changes weekly and might include tortelli with nettles in nut sauce, *pappardelle* with hare sauce, or ravioli filled with rabbit and thyme.

⑪ Antica Trattoria da Guido, Via Madonna del Prato 85, **T** 0575 23760. *Mon-Sat 1230-1430, 1930-2230*. Intimate feel at this restaurant with warm yellow walls in the historic centre of the city. The hand-written menu might include a good selection of *crostini*, Tuscan-style tripe and Florentine steaks.

¶¶ Enoteca Bacco and Arianna, Via Cesalpino 10, **T** 0575 299598. *Daily 1000-2000, Thu-Sat open for dinner 1000-2200 (approx)*. This cosy *enoteca* has a frescoed ceiling and old fittings. During the day you can come and taste local cheeses and wines, while dinner features lovely seasonal food made with fresh produce. Look out for traditional specialities like pork with garlic and fennel, *pappa al pomodoro*, or *peposa alla fornacinia* – beef cooked with garlic, peppers and wine.

¶¶ Il Saraceno, Via Mazzini 6a, **T** 0575 27644. *Thu-Tue 1200-1500, 1900-2230, closed most of Jan and Jul*. Simple *trattoria* with a relaxed atmosphere: sepia photos, walls lined with shelves stacked with wine, large bottles of olive oil on the tables. Dishes might include ravioli with ricotta and spinach, or lamb with rosemary.

¶ Caffè dei Costanti, Piazza San Francesco 19, **T** 0575 21660. *Tue-Sun 0800-2200*. The walls of this historic café are lined with mirrors, though the interior's less ornate than you might expect from the outside. As well as locals drinking espressos at the bar, you'll also find lots of tourists, as the café featured in the film *Life is Beautiful*.

¶ Coffee o'Clock, Corso Italia 184, **T** 0575 333067. *0800-2000*. Refreshing contemporary café with stripped floors, shiny counters and a large table strewn with papers and magazines. Serves hot drinks and snacks.

¶ Da Memmo, Via Cavour 70, Piazza della Badia, **T** 0575 23563. *Mon-Sat 0900-2400*. Café that also sells light meals, including fish. Selection of Neapolitan desserts.

¶ L'Agania, Via Mazzini 10, **T** 0575 295381. *Tue-Sun 1200-1500, 1900-late*. Red and white checked tablecloths and walls give this *trattoria* a vibrant look. Serves hard-to-find Tuscan dishes and unusual cuts of meat like pigs' trotters and veal cheeks, as well as rabbit, duck and wild boar.

¶ **La Torre**, Corso Italia 102, **T** 0575 24728. *Tue-Fri 1200-2100, Sat and Sun 1200-2400*. This café's worth a visit for the features preserved inside. Glass sections of the floor reveal parts of an old Roman wall and pits once used to store wheat. There's also a little terrace reached by stairs at the back of the café.

¶ **O Scugnizzo**, Via Redi 9. *Tue-Sun 1930-2330*. Terracotta walls and good Neapolitan pizzas at low prices. As well as standard sizes they also serve 1-m-wide pizzas – to share of course.

¶ **Vineria L'Ocanda**, Via Ricasoli 36, **T** 0575 351183. *1130-1730, 1900-late*. Clean and contemporary wine bar opposite the Duomo, with stone floors and cane chairs. They also serve food including tasty *crostini* and specialities such as *lardo di Arnad* (pork fat from the Val d'Aosta). Good value.

Paradiso, Piazza Guido Monaco. *Apr-Oct daily, more erratic in winter*. A *gelateria* serving some of the best ices in town.

Cortona

¶¶¶ **Osteria del Teatro**, Via Maffei 2, **T** 0575 630556. *Thu-Tue 1230-1430, 1930-2130*. A historic building, intimate dining areas and walls hung with photos of old theatrical productions, make this one of the loveliest places to eat in town. Locals come here for special occasions. The food is Tuscan with an imaginative twist, so you might find ravioli filled with pumpkin flowers, pasta with chicory and ricotta in red wine sauce, and meaty dishes like beef with *lardo di Colonnata* and plum sauce. Extensive wine list and good choice of vegetarian dishes. Booking recommended.

¶¶ Hosteria La Bucaccia, Via Ghibellina 17, **T** 0575 606039. *Apr-Nov daily for lunch and dinner, winter closed Mon*. Thick stone walls and old wine barrels at this friendly family restaurant. There's an excellent selection of *pecorino* cheeses aged from 15 to 180 days, as well as tasty *crostini* and home-made pasta served with seasonal produce such as truffles or *porcini*. Meat eaters can have beef cooked in Chianti, and veggies can opt for dishes like beans with black cabbage.

¶¶ La Locanda nel Loggiato, Piazza di Pescheria 3, **T** 0575 630575. *Thu-Tue lunch and dinner*. Picturesque setting in the centre of Cortona makes this a favourite place for both locals and tourists to eat. The menu's imaginative with options like spelt with chicory and parmesan, Val di Chiana steak with pepper and rosemary, or steak with shallots in Marsala. In late autumn you might find polenta with white truffle cream.

¶ Trattoria Dardano, Via Dardano 24, **T** 0575 601944. *Thu-Tue 1200-1445, 1915-2145*. With plain whitewashed walls and family photographs, there's a relaxed feel to this simple eaterie. The menu consists of uncomplicated Italian and Tuscan dishes – with many of the ingredients produced on the family's farm. They get pretty busy – and once even had to turn Gwyneth Paltrow away.

¶ Fufluns, Via Ghibellina 3, **T** 0575 604140. *Mar-Jan Wed-Mon 1230-1430, 1930-2300*. Fufluns' pizzas are so delicious that you'll almost certainly have to book to get in here, especially in the evening. Inside are sunny yellow tablecloths, brick and beam ceilings and a friendly bustle. They also serve pasta and fish on Fridays.

¶ **Tuscher**, Via Nazionale 43, **T** 0575 62053. *Food lunchtime only, Tue-Sun 0800-2100, till midnight in summer.* Lovely café in a historic building, furnished in restrained, contemporary style with striking artworks on the walls. Pop in for delicious fresh pasta or *bruschetta* for lunch – and leave room for desserts like chocolate pudding. Also serves creamy cappuccinos, cocktails and wine by the glass. Often have live music.

Most of Siena's nightlife is focused on its bars, which draw a mix of young locals and students, both Italian and from overseas. The novelty value – locally anyway – makes themed pubs particularly popular: there's an Aussie pub on Via di Pantaneto, and a couple of Celtic drinking dens up near the Fortezza. Early evening activity converges on Via Banchi di Sopra and the bars that ring the Campo. People later disperse to bars around the city, or to restaurants for a leisurely dinner. Some of the bars have live music. Clubs are mostly outside Siena and offer popular packages that cover dinner and dancing. The Sienese do a lot of their socializing within their own *contrada*, out of sight of visitors. Each *contrada* has its own bar and members regularly dine together. However, from late spring through to early winter, outdoor dinners are held celebrating past Palio victories. The streets of the *contrada* are decorated, temporary bars set up and everyone dresses up. Ask locally to find out if a dinner's taking place while you're there.

Piazza del Campo and around

Il Palio, Piazza Il Campo, **T** 0577 282055. *0830-0100.*
Map 2, A5, p236 The most popular spot on the Campo to sit with
a bowl of salted nuts and a pre-prandial *prosecco*. See also p125.

Key Largo, Via Rinaldini 17, **T** 0577 236339. *1830-2100.*
Map 2, A6, p236 Busy little bar serving cocktails and aperitifs.
A glass of *prosecco* costs €2.50. Get here early if you want to beat
the locals and enjoy your drinks on the balcony overlooking the
Campo. See also p125.

Terzo di San Martino

Buena Vista Social Pub, Via San Martino 31, **T** 0577 221423.
Open evenings till late. *Map 2, C9, p237* Chilled Havana sounds
and an interior crammed with Cuban-style memorabilia.

The Tea Room, Porta Giustizia 11, **T** 0577 222753. *Tue-Sun
2100-0300.* *Map 2, D6, p236* Cosy, arty little hangout squeezed
behind the Piazza del Mercato. They often have live music and
cabaret nights.

The Walkabout Pub, Via di Pantaneto 90, **T** 0577 270258,
www.walkaboutpub.it. *1200-0200.* *Map 2, C9, p237*
Noisy Ozzie pub popular with students and sports fans – they've
got football on TV. Friendly bar staff and knockout cocktails.
Happy hour is 1700-1800 and they've also got Foster's, British
beers and some Aussie wines.

Terzo di Città

Cantina in Piazza, Via Casato di Sotto 24, **T** 0577 222758. *Open Mon-Sat. Map 2, C5, p236* An *enoteca* rather than a bar, but they do an excellent selection of fresh *apperitivi* like *crostone* and bowls of tasty pasta, that you can feast on while tasting the wine.

Terzo di Camollia

Caffè Diacceto, Via Diacceto, **T** 0577 280426. *Mon-Sat 0800-2230. Map 3, G8, p239* It's a café as well as a bar, but is most popular at aperitif time, when a fashionable 20-something crowd meets here and spills onto the street outside.

Dublin Post, Piazza Gramsci 20/21, **T** 0577 289089. *Mon-Sat 1200-0200, Sun 1800-0200. Map 3, B6, p238* Sure and begorrah this is a real Italian Irish pub, with lots of dark wood and fiddle music. It's very popular with Siena's youth and tourists – it's right by the bus station – and has plenty of seats outside. Great for anyone in need of a refreshing glass of Guinness. Happy hour 1800-2100.

Il Barone Rosso, Via dei Termini 9, **T** 0577 286686, www.barone-rosso.com. *Mon-Sat 2100-0300. Map 3, E9, p239* Live music at weekends, dancing, Guinness and late night snacks – fairly funky bar in the centre of the city.

Il Cavaliere Errante, Piazza Provenzano Salvani 3, **T** 0577 280150. *Phone for opening hours. Map 3, E11, p239* Dark, atmospheric bar with foaming glasses of beer. Sometimes has live music.

Bars and clubs

I Terzi, Via dei Termini 7, **T** 0577 44329. *Tue-Sat 1100-2300.*
Map 3, E9, p239 Gets its name from the fact that it's situated at
the meeting of the 'thirds' or *terzi* of Siena. Sophisticated *enoteca*
that does a good line in aperitifs.

Kroeg, Via diPian d'Ovile 70, **T** 0577 223256. *Off Via di Vallerozzi,
not far from San Francesco church. Map 3, B10, p239* This Belgian-
style pub has a range of beer including Stella and Hoegaarden.
Plenty of seats under the brick arches where you can soak up the
booze with *panini* and pizza.

L'Officina, Piazza del Sale 3a, *Map 3, A7, p239.* Pub with live
music on Thu.

Nannini, Via Banchi di Sopra 22, **T** 0577 236009. *Mon-Sat 0730-2300,
Sun 0800-2100 (2000 in winter). Map 3, E9, p239* Popular re-fuelling
stop on the evening *passeggiata*, owned by former Formula One driver
Alessandro Nannini. Locals pop in for cocktails, wine and nibbles at the
counter. Plenty of mirrors to facilitate perfect posing.

Rock Café, Piazza Provenzano 3. *Mon, Wed, Fri and Sat 2100-0200,
Tue and Sun 2000-0100. Map 3, E11, p239* Trendy city sound bar,
it has live music and attracts a bouncy crowd of students and those
wanting a bop.

Robert the Bruce, Via Monte Santo 1, **T** 0577 285175. *Phone for
opening hours. Map 3, C1, p238 (off map)* As the name suggests, this is
a Scottish-themed pub, on the edge of the city up behind the Fortezza.
It's got a popular following with young Sienese and over 50 types of
whisky. Some British beers on offer too, including Old Peculiar,
McEwans and Newcastle Brown. Good place to mix with the locals.

San Jose, Via Cecco Angiolieri 14. *1100-0200. Map 3, F10,
p239* Pub that often has music, attracting a lively young crowd.

Around Siena

South of Siena

Il Bombo, Monteroni d'Arbia, **T** 0577 372185. *Fri and Sat evenings till late. About 20 mins' drive south of Siena*. Disco and dining is the idea here and most people dress to impress. €30 buys a meal and disco, €15 if you just want to groove. They have some separate bars serving rum and wine.

L'Angolo del Vino, Via Dante Alighieri 37, San Quirico d'Orcia, **T** 0577 897502. *Tue-Sun 0700-2400*. Popular with young people this café/wine bar serves a variety of local wines by the glass.

West of Siena

Arturo's Pub, Via XX Settembre 8, Poggibonsi. *Tue-Sun 2100-0200. North of Colle di Val d'Elsa*. They must mean Arturo Smith's pub, for this is a British-style drinking den with dark wooden floors, small round tables and a wide range of beers. Choose from Tennents, Guinness, Caffrey's and Belgian brews.

Avalon, Viale Roma 1-5, San Gimignano, **T** 0577 940023, www.avalon-pub.com. *Summer Tue-Sun 1200-0200, winter 2000-0200*. Live music sessions and a range of beers. There's an airy terrace for hot nights.

Blue Train Club, Via di Vallepiatta 18, Poggibonsi, **T** 3333 278713, www.bluetrainclub.it. *2100-late. North of Colle di Val d'Elsa*. Live blues, jazz and rock bands on Fridays and Saturdays and jam sessions on Wednesday.

Di Vinorum, Piazza Cisterna 30/A, San Gimignano, **T** 0577 907192. *1200-0100 (most days)*. Downstairs, beneath the wine shop, is this cellar bar where you can buy around 20 different wines by the glass – including the local Vernaccia. Plenty of snacks too, designed to complement the wines.

La Vena di Vino, Via Don Minzoni 30, Volterra, **T** 0588 81491. *Wed-Mon 0930-late*. Lovely, cosy little *enoteca* run by Bruno and Lucio, who serve simple, good-quality food with a good choice of wine.

Muzic, Rosia. *About 10 mins' drive southwest of Siena*. Relaxed dining and dancing in two rooms. Seats for 200 and a mix of hip-hop, R&B and disco. €5 on Friday, €12-15 on Saturday. Dinner will set you back €20.

Web and Wine, Via Porta all'Arco 11-13, Volterra, **T** 0588 81531. *Fri-Wed 0700-0100*. Great internet café that serves breakfasts, light lunches and has a wide selection of wines from around the world. Set in an ancient building, it has a glass-covered medieval grain silo in front of the bar and a section of Etruscan/Roman pavement.

East of Siena

Caffè degli Artisti, Via Nazionale 18, Cortona, **T** 0575 601237. *Phone for opening hours*. Central bar attracting everyone from locals to visiting students who come in for cocktails, Chianti and glasses of beer.

Essenza, Loc Caseta, **T** 339 7191914, www.essenzaonline.it. *7 km east of Siena on way to Arezzo*. An auditorium with restaurant and club where live bands often play as well.

La Vispa Teresa, outskirts of Arezzo, www.lavispateresa.it. *Take exit Valdichiana off A1, marked Bettolle (SI)*. Slick American bar and club outside town.

Le Mirage Disco, Vle S M Vertighe 34, Monte San Savino, **T** 0575 810215, www.lemirage.it. *South of Arezzo, just off main A1*. Various dance anthems and some live music.

Le Tastevin, Via de Cenci 9, **T** 0575 28304, *Tue-Sun 1230-1430, 1930-2330*. This is a *trattoria*/jazz bar. The bar is lined with images of film stars and the owner often plays jazz here at the weekends. You can sit outside in summer.

Lions Well Pub, Piazza Signorelli, Cortona, **T** 0575 604918. *Evenings from around 2100, closed Tue*. Cosy, stone-walled pub in the centre of Cortona. Very popular with young locals, who come for the novelty of drinking beer. There's sometimes music playing too.

Route 66, Via Nazionale, Cortona, **T** 0575 62727. *Phone for opening hours*. This is a pub/pizzeria that attracts a young crowd. There's sometimes live music playing.

Vineria, L'Ocanda, Via Ricasoli 36, Arezzo, **T** 0575 351183. *1130-1730, 1900-late*. Clean and contemporary wine bar opposite the Duomo, with stone floors and cane chairs. They also serve food.

Vita Bella, Piazza San Francesco 22. Arezzo. *Thu-Tue 0900-0100*. A good time to call in to this small café/bar is around 1800, when you can join locals enjoying a selection of aperitifs.

More provincial than Florence, Siena isn't noted for having a thriving arts scene. Italians from outside the city often complain that they are interested in nothing but the Palio and life in the *contrade*. Certainly the Palio is the most important event in the city (see Festivals), and preparations for it occupy much of local people's time.

The most important arts events are musical. Classical concerts are organized by the prestigious Accademia Musicale Chigiana and staged at various venues. The long Italian tradition of movie-going is apparent with several cinemas screening both Italian and foreign-language films. There's also a lively complement of student film-makers at the university. A variety of plays and dance events, both traditional and contemporary, are staged at the city's theatres, while surrounding towns like Volterra, with its historic Persio Flacca theatre, and Arezzo, which has several cinemas, are also worth checking out. Posters advertising concerts and other events in Siena are often pasted up around Piazza Matteotti.

Cinema

The Italian film industry has an illustrious history and from early
days featured real locations and landscapes, which gave the films
a distinctive and memorable quality. Italian directors are known all
over the world, the lengthy list including Luchini Visconti, Roberto
Rossellini, Federico Fellini, Bernardo Bertolucci and Roberto
Benigni. Siena's Palio has been the inspiration for some films,
including *Palio* (1932) by Alessandro Blasetti, *The Love Specialist*
(1957) by Luigi Zampa and *The Last Victory* (2004) a documentary
film by Nathaniel Kahn. The city has two film festivals each year,
one specializing in short films (p174).

   The beauty of the landscape and the exceptional quality of
the light mean that the countryside around Siena is often used
by film-makers. Shakespeare's comedies have been given cheerful
Tuscan settings: Chianti in Kenneth Branagh's *Much Ado About
Nothing* (1993), and Montepulciano in *A Midummer Night's Dream*
(1998, Michael Hoffman) starring Michelle Pfeiffer and Kevin Kline.
The hill towns and picture-perfect landscapes of the Val d'Orcia
have attracted everyone from Ridley Scott, who shot part of
Gladiator (2000) here, to Anthony Minghella, who memorably
used the frescoed refectory of Sant'Anna in Camprena in *The
English Patient* (1996). San Gimignano's medieval towers were a
favourite of Franco Zeffirelli, who substituted them for Assisi in
Brother Sun, Sister Moon (1971) and later formed the setting for
Tea with Mussolini (1999) starring Maggie Smith and Judi Dench.
Films often spark a tourist boom. Arezzo attracts lots of people
keen to see locations featured in *Life is Beautiful* (1997, Roberto
Benigni), and Cortona sometimes seems swamped by visitors
on the *Under the Tuscan Sun* (2003, Audrey Wells) trail.

Siena

Siena has several cinemas often showing foreign films in the original language. Tickets cost around €6.70, concessions around €5.20. Afternoon showings are sometimes cheaper at €4.

Cineforum, Piazza dell'Abbadia 6, **T** 0577 283044. *Map 3, D9, p239*

Cinema Nuovo Pendolo, Via San Quirico 13, **T** 0577 43012, www.cinemanuovopendolo.it. *Map 2, F2, p236* Art house films.

Fiamma, Via di Pantaneto 141, **T** 0577 284503. *Map 2, C9, p237*

Impero, Via Vittorio Emanuele II 14, **T** 0577 48260. *Off map*

Metropolitan, Piazza G Matteotti, **T** 0577 47109. *Map 3, D7, p239*

Moderno, Via Calzoleria 44, just off Piazza Tolomei, **T** 0577 289201. *Map 3, F10, p239* A short film on the Palio is shown here from April to October, Monday to Saturday. It lasts 20 minutes and screenings take place in several languages including English. Leaflets are available from the tourist office.

Odeon, Via Banchi di Sopra 31, **T** 0577 48260. *Map 3, E9, p239*

Arezzo

Europlex, Via Turati 2, **T** 0575 334300, www.europlexcinemas.it, *out of town*, **Multisala Corso**, Corso Italia 115, **T** 0575 24883, and **Supercinema**, Via Garibaldi 101, **T** 0575 22834, all screen mainstream films.

Multisala Eden, Via Guadagnoli 2, **T** 0575 35364. More arty and original-language films.

Comedy

There's no great tradition of stand up comedy in the city – but look out for Manfred, the German with the red hat, who entertains diners on the Campo most days during the summer months. He's been going to Siena for years and is now part of the local scene.

Dance

Both contemporary and classical works are staged at the **Teatro dei Rozzi**, Piazza Independenza 15, **T** 0577 46960. *Map 2, A4, p236* This is also the location for a charity dance event held each June, organized by **Centro Studio Danza**, Via B Tolomei 7, **T** 0577 51780, www.sienadanza.it.

Music

Accademia Musicale Chigiana, Via di Città 89, **T** 0577 22091, www.chigiana.it. *Map 2, C4, p236* This, the most prestigious musical establishment in Siena, is housed in the medieval **Palazzo Chigi Saracini** and was founded in 1932 by Count Guido Chigi Saracini. It has a concert season from November to March, known as the *Micat in Vertice* – the Saracini family's motto. In July it organizes the *Settimana Musicale Senese*, a week of concerts featuring both celebrated and lesser-known classical works. Concerts also take place during the summer months.

Chiesa Anglicana, Via Garibaldi 32, **T** 340 8119192. *Map 3, A7, p239 (off map)* Classical concerts are also often held this church. Check the Tourist Office for information.

Theatre

Siena

Siena's greatest theatre is of course the Campo, in which the city's most theatrical event, the Palio, is staged. The Campo also acts like a theatre every day, as all the dramas of city life seem to be played out here. The city has a range of theatres staging all types of performances, from traditional classics to more contemporary works.

Piccolo Teatro, Via dei Montanini 118, **T** 0577 281190. *Map 3, C7, p239*

Teatro dei Rinnovati, Piazza del Campo 1, **T** 0577 292265. *Map 1, H4, p234*

Teatro dei Rozzi, Piazza Independenza 15, **T** 0577 46960. *Map 3, G9, p239*

Volterra

Teatro Persio Flacco, Via dei Sarti 37-39, **T** 0588 88204, www.fts.toscana.it.   Built in 1819 this is a small but exquisite version of an opera house with plush velvet upholstery and rich gilding. Once used for dress rehearsals of operas to be staged at La Scala, now restored and used for concerts and theatrical performances.

Arezzo

Teatro Petrarca, Via Guido Monaco 10, **T** 0575 23975.

Teatro Comunale della Bicchieraia, Via della Bicchieraia 32, **T** 0575 302258, www.comune.arezzo.it/stagioneprosa.

Cortona

Teatro Signorelli, Piazza Signorelli, **T** 0575 601882, www.teatrosignorelli.com.   Variety of theatre, music and cinema.

Arts and entertainment

Siena's most important event is without doubt the Palio, the bareback horse race that's run every year in the Campo. It's colourful, wild and brutal. The whole city pours onto the streets and there's hardly room to breathe, let alone move. Tourists flood in to watch, paying high prices for the scarce seats – though it's free if you stand in the Campo. Many agencies offer to find seats if you are determined to go. The Palio's televised now – but many Sienese resent this intrusion and don't really want tourists there either: the Palio is theirs and theirs alone. It's living history.

Traditional celebrations are still a vital part of Tuscan life. Most take place in summer and autumn and many of them are focused on local food and wine. Harvest time sees festivals celebrating everything from chestnuts to olive oil. Food's often cooked outdoors and everyone spills onto the streets to join in. They're a great opportunity to experience village life. Festivals often have a historic theme too, with processions, medieval costumes and hotly contested tournaments.

All year

Antique Fair, (Arezzo, the first Sunday of every month, and the preceding Saturday), www.arezzoantiquefair.com. More than 500 exhibitors spread throughout Arezzo for the city's monthly fair.

March

Fiera di San Giuseppe (Siena, 19 March). Celebration of the Contrada dell'Onda's (Wave) patron saint. This is an outdoor fair with stalls selling traditional fritters and handmade toys. The focus is on the children of the *contrada*.

May

Giostra dell'Archidado (Cortona). Period costumes and processions at this crossbow competition which dates back to 1397.

June

Festa del Barbarossa (San Quirico d'Orcia, 3rd Sun in June). Medieval festival of flag waving and crossbow competitions.

Giostra del Saracino (Arezzo, penultimate Saturday of June, in the evening, and first Sunday of September, in the afternoon). Historic joust and procession, all in medieval costume. Winners of the tournament get the Golden Lance.

July

Il Palio (Siena, 2 July). See box, p170. The first of the Palios, takes place at 1930 in the Campo. Ten *contrade* race in it. Trials are run on 29 June at 1930, 30 June at 0900 and 1930, 1 July at 0900, 2 July at 0900. There is a dress rehearsal on 1 July at 1930. At 1530 on

The Palio

"For us the Palio is a play"
(member of one of Siena's
contrade, 2004)

Rivalry, intrigue, pageantry,
bribery and brutality – the
Palio has it all. The origins of
this spectacle possibly go back
to the 13th century, when a
feast and horse race were held
giving thanks to the Madonna
for Siena's victory at Montaperti
in 1260. The first documented
Palio was in 1310, though the
race has evolved over the
centuries. It's a bareback horse
race, a bitterly contested
contest between the various
contrade in which old scores are
settled – and anything goes. It's
held in the Campo and involves
three circuits of the 'shell'.

There are actually two Palios:
the first held on 2nd July, the
second on 16th August. Ten out
of the 17 *contrade* take part in
each one (there's no room for
more). Seven are guaranteed a
place if they missed the July race
the preceeding year, and the
other three are drawn by lots. A
week before the race the
Campo's covered with earth, *la
terra in piazza*, to create the
track. In the run up to the race
a lot of dealing – and double
dealing – goes on. The jockeys
are all outsiders, often from the
Maremma, and can earn large
sums of money from the race.
Captains of the *contrade*
negotiate to get the best rider
for their district, but jockeys also
do deals between one another.
Ten horses are also chosen.

Three days before the race,
there is a public draw to assign
the horses from the pool to the
competing districts: once
allotted they can't be changed.
The horses are then led to
special stalls within their
contrada and are placed under
24-hour guard to prevent
doping. The jockeys, who aren't
held in much respect by the
locals, are also kept under
close watch. On the day of the
race the horse and jockey are
blessed in the relevant
contrada church. The race is
preceded by a parade, with

contrada members dressed in medieval costumes, waving flags and beating drums. The Campo fills with people (crowds of 30,000 to 40,000 fill Siena on race days) and tension heightens. The jockeys continue making deals between themselves on the starting line – and scramble for position. Once the race begins it's a mêlée, riders can beat one another and their horses – and if jockeys fall off it doesn't matter, the horse that finishes first is the winner, riderless or not. Although mattresses are placed at certain points to provide protection – notably at the tight San Martino curve – the race is dangerous, particularly for the horses. Injured horses receive good veterinary care, but around 50 have died in the last 30 odd years; fewer than in Britain's *Grand National* but still a large number. Although crime hardly exists in Siena (the *contrada* system sees to that), fights often break out on race days, generally between members of rival *contrade* and a lot of alcohol is consumed. Married couples from different *contrade* tend to stay away from one another at the Palio – it avoids tension.

Once the race is over – and it only lasts around 90 seconds, the celebrations begin. The next best thing to winning the race is seeing your rival lose it. The winning *contrada* becomes the 'baby' and members wear dummies round their necks – you'll frequently see this around the city long after the Palio is over. The one that hasn't won for longest becomes the *nonna*, or grandmother.

A dinner is held by the winning *contrada* – the horse being the star guest. In the months after the race, victory dinners continue to be held outdoors and preparations begin for the next Palio. Yet for all the pageantry the race is just the tip of the iceberg, it is the *contrade* that are the soul of Siena, not the Palio.

2 July is the blessing of the horse in each *contrada*'s church, the pageant begins around 1600 and enters the Campo at 1720 – places in the Campo start to fill up early in the day.

Volterra Teatro (lasts 10-15 days) www.volterrateatro.it. International theatre festival in Volterra. Performances throughout the city.

Festival of Val d'Orcia (July and continues into August). Theatre and music at venues throughout the Val d'Orcia.

Incontri in Terra di Siena (Siena). Music concerts performed in the Val d'Orcia, particularly at La Foce estate, www.lafoce.com.

Palio delle Contrade (Casole d'Elsa, 2nd Sunday of July) casolani@casole.it. Horse race between town *contrade* and festivities spread over a week.

Chianti Festival (Chianti towns) **T** 0577 738791, info@chianti festival.it. 10-day art festival in towns of Castellina in Chianti, Castelnuovo Berardenga, Gaiole in Chianti and Radda in Chianti.

Siena Jazz (Siena and nearby towns and villages, late July and early August). Fortezza Medicea **T** 0577 271401, www.sienajazz.it, organize the Siena Jazz Festival. Sessions take place in locations within the city centre and in nearby towns and villages. Events are often free of charge.

August

Il Palio (Siena, 16 August). See box, p170. This is the second of the Palios. The race takes place at 1900. Those *contrade* that have not already raced, plus three more, take part. Trials are held on 13 August at 0900 and 1900, 14 August at 0900 and 1900, 15 August at 0900, 16 August at 0900. There is a dress rehearsal on 15 August at 1900. Blessing of the horses takes place at 1500 in *contrade* churches on 16 August, the procession enters the Campo at 1650.

Cortonantiquaria (Cortona, August and early September). The oldest antique furniture fair in Italy with over 40 dealers coming to the little town.

Sagra della Bistecca (Cortona). Outdoor food fest celebrating the local Valdichiana beef.

Bruscello (Montepulciano, 14, 15 and 16 August). Actors re-enact events in the town's history.

Bravio delle Botti (Montepulciano, last Sunday in August). A lively challenge between the town's eight *contrade*. Heavy barrels are rolled uphill through the centre – the winner receiving a cloth banner (*bravio*). It dates back to 1373. Events are preceded by a week of celebrations.

September

Palio della Balestra (Sansepolcro). Medieval crossbow competition between teams from Sansepolcro and Gubbio.

Siena Film Festival (Siena, end September to early October) **T** 0577 222999, www.sienafilmfestival.it. The city hosts an increasingly popular festival showing a variety of films including Italian and foreign comedies.

October

Chestnut Festival (Castiglione d'Orcia, last Sunday in October). Lots of chances to taste dishes made from the local chestnuts; particularly focused on the hamlets of Vivo and Campiglia.

Tartufo Bianco (Volterra, late October early November). Special white truffle market. There are lots of stalls in the village selling the celebrated white truffles.

November

Mostra del Tartufo Bianco delle Crete Senesi (San Giovanni d'Asso, second and third weekends of November). White truffle festival. The village fills up with stalls selling local white truffles, as well as other fresh local produce and crafts. There's a large tent where hot dishes are sold and restaurants feature truffles on their menus.

Siena International Short Film Festival (Siena). www.corto italiacinema.com. For one week this event, 10 years old in 2005, screens short films, animations and documentaries from around the world – a different theme each year. It also showcases work made by students of Siena's university and has special films for children.

December

Festa dell'Olio (San Quirico d'Orcia, first weekend in December). Olive oil festival. There are lots of stalls giving you the chance to taste the new season's olive oil (a bit like trying the new Beaujolais), as well as street bands.

Fiera di Santa Lucia (Siena, 13 December). Feast day of St Lucia, celebrations focused on the Contrada della Chiocciola (Snail). The streets are filled with market stalls selling food and traditional crafts.

!
• Flag waving forms part of the pageantry of the Palio and you will often see young Sienese boys perfecting their skills in the streets of their *contrada*.

You can shop till your credit card squeals in Siena. The city's crammed with everything from big-name clothes stores like Max Mara to small workshops producing stained glass and ceramics. It's not the place to come for bargains – many young Sienese shop for everyday clothes in Poggibonisi – but the quality of goods is extremely high. Handmade, *fatto a mano*, goods are a speciality, and the techniques are often the same as those used for centuries. You can find anything here from designer knickers and tailored trousers, to olive-wood salad bowls, handmade paper and ceramics colourfully decorated with *contrade* symbols.

There are also plenty of tempting delis, bakeries, food stores and wine shops filled with all the local specialities you've been savouring. Whether you want a bottle of Brunello, some organic olive oil, or a piece of *panforte*, you'll find it here.

The main shopping streets are Via Banchi di Sopra and Via di Città. Hours are generally 0930-1300 and 1500-1900, and shops often close on Monday. Shoppers resident outside the EU can claim tax refunds on their purchases.

Siena

Some of Siena's shops are like mini museums. The pharmacy on Il Campo, for instance, is 700 years old and has a stunning Liberty-style interior, the walls lined with exquisite lacquered panels. And Benetton, Via Banchi di Sopra 54, has some unexpected and exuberant 16th-century frescoes on the ceiling, a legacy of the building's days as a bank.

Art

Alvalenti, Via di Beccheria, **T** 0577 286888. *Usually open daily. Map 2, A4, p236* Popular cartoon *contrade* posters. The artists will also do personalized works relating to your job, favourite animal, etc.

Biale Cerruti Art Gallery, Via di Città 111, **T** 0577 223793, *Mon-Sat 1030-2000. Map 2, B4, p236* Contemporary art from all over Italy, including works by Tuscan artists.

Books and paper

La Parpagliola, Via di Città 79, **T** 0577 281144. *Mon-Sat summer 1030-1930, winter 1030-1330, 1500-1930, usually closed Jan and Feb. Map 2, B4, p236* **Il Papiro**, Via di Città 37, **T** 0577 284241. *0930-1930. Map 2, B4, p236* Both sell lovely books and diaries made from handmade paper.

Libreria Senese, Via di Città 64, **T** 0577 280845. *Mon-Sat 0900-2000, Sun 1000-2000. Map 2, B4, p236* Handy bookshop with lots of English-language titles, as well as good selection of Italian works. Foreign-language newspapers too, if you need day-old news from home.

Clothes

Cortecci, Via Banchi di Sopra 27, **T** 0577 280096 (*0930-2000*) *Map 3, G9, p239*, and Il Campo 30, **T** 0577 280984 (*1000-1300, 1530-2000*) *Map 2, B5, p236* Designer heaven with enough labels to please both the Beckhams. Gucci, Armani and Cavalli on Banchi di Sopra, and Dolce e Gabbana, Alberte Ferretti and Dries-Van-Noten on Il Campo.

Dolci Trame, Via del Moro 4, **T** 0577 46168. *Tue-Sat 1000-1300, 1530-1930, Mon 1530-1930. Just off Piazza Tolomei. Map 3, F10, p239* Friendly staff and good range of quirky designer clothes for women. Ideal for something a bit different.

Futuro's, Via dei Montanini 65, **T** 0577 281080. *Mon-Sat 0900-1300, 1530-1930. Map 3, D8, p239* Slighty intimidating shop stocked with women's designer clothes. Not for fat days.

Furla, Via di Città 6-8, **T** 0577 281287. *Mon-Sat 1000-2000. Map 2, B4, p236* Covetable handbags and watches.

Il Cashmere, Via di Città 47, **T** 0577 47755. *Mon-Sat 1000-1330, 1500-1930. Map 2, B4, p236* The clue's in the name – lots of lovely soft cashmere.

Il Telaio, Chiasso del Bargello 2, **T** 0577 47065. *Mon-Sat 0930-1930. Map 2, B4, p236* Classic clothes with a twist. The name means the 'loom', and dresses, jackets, coats and scarves are all woven by hand. A tad pricier than Primark but then it'll last forever.

L'Angolo della Maglia, Via della Sapienza 50, **T** 0577 287866. *Mon-Sat 1000-1300, 1600-1930. Map 3, E7, p239* Jumpers in wool and mohair, handmade locally.

★ **Things to bring home**

Best
- Handmade crafts, p180
- Your favourite wine, p181
- Fresh olive oil, p181
- Almondy *ricciarelli*, p183
- Rich slabs of *panforte*, p183

Look & Moda, Via San Pietro 15, **T** 0577 280514. *Mon-Sat 0930-1300, 1545-1945. Map 2, E3, p236* Exclusive Italian designer womenswear. Stock names like Atos Lombardini, Blu Time and Dream.

New Shop Boutique, Via dei Montanini 104, **T** 0577 286294. *Tue-Sat 0900-1300, 1530-1930. Map 3, D7, p239* Not for the scruffy. Immaculate little shop stocking labels like Paul Smith, Hussein Chalayan and Gibo.

Palumbo, Via San Pietro 1/5, **T** 0577 40406. *Summer daily 1000-1300, 1600-2000 , winter Tue-Fri 1000-1300, 1530-1930, Sat 1000-1300. Map 2, E3, p236* Original women's clothes, with unusual jackets and pretty tops.

Ragno, just off Via di Calzoleria. *Tue-Sat. Map 2, A5, p236* Old-fashioned little shop stuffed with all sorts of loose buttons, braiding, sequins, etc. Long queues; it's very popular with local women chatter.

Stefano Veneziani, Via dei Montanini 86, **T** 0577 45860. *Tue-Sat 0930-1300, 1530-1930, Mon 1530-1930 only. Map 3, D7, p239* Smart men's clothes store, stocking things like cashmere jumpers.

Shopping

Tessuti a Mano, Via San Pietro 7, **T** 0577 282200. *Mon-Fri, sometimes Sat 1030-1900. Map 2, E3, p236* Lovely shop with all sorts of handmade items, like jumpers, hats and ponchos in silk, mohair and wool. They've also got perky little bags at around €35.

TT, Via Banchi di Sopra, **T** 0577 43926. *Tue-Sat. Map 3, G9, p239* Shoes and pricey handbags.

Crafts and ceramics

Alessandro Marchionni, Via San Pietro 22. *Map 2, E3, p236* Distinctive handmade ceramics: some with *contrade* symbols, some inspired by the floor of the Duomo.

Ceramiche di Santa Caterina, Via di Città 74/76, **T** 0577 283098. *1000-2000. Map 2, B4, p236* Good-quality ceramics. Many still come for the distinctive cups used in the film *Mrs Doubtfire*.

Il Pellicano, Via Diacetto 17 (shop) and Vicolo di Vallepiatta 4 (workshop), **T** 0577 247914. *Spring and summer daily 1030-1930, rest of the year Mon-Sat 1030-1300, 1530-1930. Map 2, A3, p236* Lovely handmade ceramics in fresh, cheery colours.

La Bottega delle Cere, Via di Pantaneto 103, **T** 0577 40703 (*Mon-Sat 1000-1330, 1600-1900*), *Map 2, B8, p237*; **La Fabbrica delle Candele**, Via dei Pellegrini, **T** 0577 236417 (*Fri-Wed 0930-1930*), *Map 2, B3, p236*; **La Fabbrica delle Candele**, Via dei Pellegrini, **T** 0577 236417 (*Fri-Wed 0930-1930*) *Map 2, B3, p236* All three are good for decorated candles.

Luciana Staderini, Via Monna Agnese, **T** 0577 43316. *Open when it's open. Map 2, C3, p236* Studio of a local sculptress tucked behind the Duomo.

> ### Strings and things

Be prepared for the critically appraising looks of slim-hipped staff when buying lingerie. The underwear is often hidden away, cruelly forcing you to admit your size to the assistant – who tends to repeat it loudly, or even correct you. Try **Infore**, Via da Città 7 (*Mon-Sat 0930-1945*); **Intimissimi**, Via Piangiani (*daily*); **Yamamay**, Via Banchi di Sopra 61/63, **T** 0577 222644 (*Mon-Sat 0930-1930, Sun 1530-1930*). For posh knickers like Dolce and Gabbana and Roberto Cavalli make for **Barbara**, Via dei Montanini 81, **T** 0577 280848, (*Mon-Sat 0900-1300, 1530-1930*). **Marzia**, Banchi di Sotto 6, **T** 0577 223109 (*Mon-Sat 0930-1300, 1530-2000*), also stocks men's underwear and sells La Perla and Dolce and Gabbana.

Vetrate Artistiche, Via della Galluzza, **T** 0577 48033. *Mon-Fri 0900-1300, 1500-1800. Map 2, A3, p236* Fascinating stained-glass workshop. They do commissions for a variety of buildings, and also sell small items like earrings, photo frames and bracelets.

Food and drink

Cantina in Piazza, Via Casato di Sotto 24, **T** 0577 222758. *Mon-Sat. Map 2, C5, p236* Five rooms laden with Italian wines. You can buy a decent bottle of Chianti for €15 or splurge on the finest Brunello for €450.

Consorzio Agrario Siena, Via Pianigiani 9, **T** 0577 47449. *Mon-Sat 0800-1930. Map 3, D8, p239* Deli/supermarket with good range of Sienese and Tuscan produce. Lots of wine, honey, biscuits, and dried *porcini* – as well as basics for a picnic.

Drogheria Manganelli, Via di Città 71-73, **T** 0577 280002. *Daily. Map 2, B4, p236* Ancient pharmacy, now a swish food shop. The old glass-fronted cabinets are filled with Italian wines and chandeliers hang from the ceiling – a clue that this isn't the place for a bargain.

Enoteca San Domenico, Via del Paradiso 56, **T** 0577 271181. *0900-2000. Map 3, E6, p238 Near San Domenico church.* Local foods and wines including *vin santo* at €13.90.

Forno dei Galli, 45 Via dei Termini, **T** 0577 289073. *Mon-Sat 0730-2000. Map 3, E9, 239* One of Siena's best bakeries.

Giusti Continentali, Via dei Rossi 107, **T** 0577 236640. *0730-2000. Map 3, D10, p239* Contemporary shop with enticing selection of fine chocolates and speciality foods from around the world.

Il Magnifico, Via dei Pellegrini 27, **T** 0577 281106. *Mon-Sat 0700-1430, 1600-1930. Map 2, B3, p236* Bakery where you can pick up freshly made *panforte* and *ricciarelli*.

Morbidi, 75 Via Banchi di Sopra 73, **T** 0577 280268. *Mon-Fri 0900-2000, Sat 0830-2000. Map 3, E9, p239* Exclusive food shop with all sorts of tasty cheeses, pastas and meats, as well as lovely honey, olive oil and treats to take home.

Panificio Moderno, Via dei Montanini 84, **T** 0577 280104. *Mon-Sat 0730-1930. Map 3, C7, p239* For freshly made *panforte* and delicious, almondy *ricciarelli*.

Homeware

Chianti Shine, Via dei Termini 49, **T** 0577 49781. *Mon-Sat 0930-1930, Sat 0930-1230 (approx). Map 3, E9, p239* Gorgeous bed linens, fabric bags and striking ceramics.

Muzzi Sergio, Via dei Termini 97, **T** 0577 40439. *Tue-Sat 0900-1300, 1530-1930, Mon 1530-1930. Map 3, E9, p239* Vases, china and sleek Alessi kitchenware.

Paglia e Fiena, Via di Città, **T** 0577 226120. *1000-1930. Map 2, B4, p236* Kitchenwares like olive wood salad bowls.

Samarcanda, Via Giovanni Duprè 14, **T** 0577 46059. *Mon-Sat 1100-1930. Map 2, C5, p236* Ethnic goods from all over the world, including unique pieces of jewellery, bags, furniture – even wall hangings from Mali.

Siena Ricama, Via di Città 64, **T** 0577 288339. *Mon-Fri 1000-1300, 1700-1930, Sat 1000-1300. Map 2, B4, p236* Embroidered lampshades inspired by historical artworks. The owner takes great pride in her work; no food or drink allowed.

Jewellery

Abracadabra, Via di Pantaneto 103b, **T** 0577 247719. *Mon-Sat 0930- 2000. Map 2, B8, p237* Lots of silver jewellery, much of it from Arezzo.

La Cocinella, Via dei Montanini 77, **T** 0577 271463. *Tue-Sun 0930-1300, 1600-1945, Mon 1600-1945. Map 3, D7, p239* If bling's your thing then have a peek in this shop specializing in handmade jewellery. Some unusual watches, lots of amber and a few rings that would double as knuckle dusters.

Markets

General Market, Viale XXV Aprile. *Every Wed 0730-1400.*
In front of the Fortezza. Map 3, D3, p238 Lively market packed
with stalls selling everything from olives to overcoats.

Antique Market, Piazza del Mercato. *3rd Sun of every month (not
Aug or over Easter), dawn till dusk. Map 2, C6, p236* Also known as
Collector's Corner, traders come to sell antiques and collectibles.
Good for browsing if not bargains.

Around Siena

Montepulciano

Aliseda, Via dell'Opio nel Corso, **T** 0578 758672. *Tue-Sun winter
1000-1300, 1600-2000, summer 0930-2000.* Handmade Etruscan-
inspired jewellery. There's a little workshop on the premises and
they'll do specially commissioned pieces.

Bottega del Rame, shop Via dell'Opio nel Corso 64, **T** 0578
758753, and workshop next to Teatro Poliziano. *Open mornings
and from 1330-1930, closed early Feb.* Signor Mazzeti makes all
sorts of lovely copper goods in this workshop. The saucepans,
lined with tin, are of very high quality.

Il Grifo e il Leone, Via di Voltaia nel Corso 33, **T** 0578 758799.
Summer 1000-1900, winter 1000-1300, 1500-1900. Pretty handmade
cups and saucers and plenty of crystal.

Maledetti Toscani, Via di Voltaia nel Corso 40, **T** 0578 757130.
Mon-Sat 1000-1900. Handmade journals and diaries, leatherware
and handmade shoes.

Outlet shopping

Fashionistas should make a pilgrimage to one of the designer discount outlet stores, www.outletfirenze.com, easily reached by car from Siena (and more easily still from Arezzo). Get there early and be prepared for a scrum.

The Mall, Via Europa 8, Leccio Reggello, **T** 055 865 7775. *Mon-Sat 1000-1900, Sun 1500-1900*. By public transport, take a train from Arezzo to Montevarchi, then a taxi. Outlet shops include **Gucci**, **Armani**, **Ferragamo**, **Yves St Laurent** and **Fendi**.

Dolce e Gabbana, Loc Santa Maria Maddalena 49, Plan dell'Isola Rignano Sull'Arno, **T** 055 8331300. *Mon-Sat 0900-1900, Sun 1500-1900*.

Prada, Strada Statale 69, Montevarchi, **T** 055 91 901, *Mon-Sat 0930-1930, Sun 1000-1300, 1400-2000*.

Pratesi, Via Dante Alighieri 83, Ambra. *Apr-Oct Mon-Sat 0900-1930, Nov-early Jan Mon-Sat 0900-1230, 1530-1900, closed Jan-end Feb*, www.shoes-pratesi.com. For shoes.

Porta della Cavina, Via di Gracciano del Corso 1/3, **T** 0578 758210. *Mon-Sat 0900-1300, 1500-2000*. Reproduction Etruscan earthenware vases.

Pienza

La Luna nel Pozza, Via Condotti 1, **T** 0578 748073. *Summer daily 0930-1300, 1530-1930, winter Mon-Sat*. Traditional local crafts including ceramics and intricate lace.

Montalcino

Arte Orafa, Piazza del Popolo 4, **T** 0577 847092. *Mon-Sat 0900-1300, 1600-2000*. Distinctive handmade jewellery.

San Quirico d'Orcia

L'Angolo di Terracotta, Via Mazzini 2, **T** 0577 839011. *Mon-Sat 1000-1900*. Workshop producing handmade ceramics.

Milletrame, Via Romana 23, Torrenieri northwest of San Qurico d'Orcia **T** 0577 834078. *Mon-Fri 0900-1230, 1430-1930, Sat 0900-1230, call before arriving*. Workshop producing lovely sheets, cushions, towels and clothes made from hemp.

Colle di Val d'Elsa

Boreno Cigni, Vicolo delle Fontanelle, **T** 0577 920326. *No set hours*. Traditional workshop producing high-quality crystal and glass.

Mezzetti, Via Oberdan 13, **T** 0577 920395. *Tue-Sat 0900-1300, 1530-1930*. Large crystal shop. Look for items from the Calp factory – considered the best.

San Gimignano

Franco Baronti, Piazzetta della Madonna 1, **T** 0522 950844. *Tue-Sun*. Homewares. Traditional ironwork in small workshop. All sorts of things from door knockers to tongs. If it's shut just call the number on the door and someone will come.

Volterra

Artieri Alabastro, Piazza dei Priori 5, **T** 0588 87590. Shop selling items made by a co-operative of alabaster craftsmen.

Cercando L'Oro, Via Guarnacci 55, **T** 0588 81500. Original pieces in gold and silver, in traditional and contemporary designs.

Fabula Etrusca, Via Lungo le Mura del Mandorlo 10, **T** 0588 87401. *Summer daily 0930-1930, winter Mon-Sat 0930-1300, 1500-1930*. Handmade gold jewellery inspired by Etruscan pieces.

Gloria Gianelli, Via di Sotto 2, **T** 0588 84030. Watch alabaster vases and plates being made.

Legatoria Artistica, Via Porta all'Arco. *Mon-Fri 1000-1300, 1600-1900, Sat 1000-1300*. Run by twin sisters this shop sells handmade books and paper. They'll do books to order too.

Spartaco Montagnani, Via Porta all'Arco 6, **T** 0588 86184. *Mon-Sat 1000-1800*. Lovely bronze Etruscan-style statuettes, handmade at this old workshop. Good place to pick up a reproduction of the *Ombra della Sera*, Volterra's ancient symbol.

Chianti

Katy at Casa San Giuseppe, Via Val di Sambra, near Castelnuovo Berardenga, **T** 0577 355436. *Mon-Sat 0900-1200, 1430-1900*. Katy works from a studio in part of this villa, producing beautiful stained-glass windows, Tiffany lamps, and unusual glassware.

Arezzo

Antique Fair, Arezzo, p169.

Busatti, Corso Italia 48, **T** 0575 355295. *Tue-Sat 0900-1300, 1530-1930, Mon 1530-1930*. Lovely hand-woven linens – locals come here to stock up on sheets, tablecloths and napkins. You can also visit their workshop, out of town at Via Mazzini 14, Anghiari, **T** 0575 788013, www.busatti.com.

Enoteca Bacco and Arianna, Via Cesalpino 10, **T** 0575 299598. *1000-2000*. There are 900 different wines for sale here. They'll show you the cellars if you wish and you can taste Tuscan wines by the glass.

Siena's got reasonable facilities for all the usual sporting and leisure activities, with swimming pools, gyms and tennis courts. However, with all that stunning Tuscan countryside to explore you're unlikely to want to spend your time pounding a treadmill indoors. Walking and cycling are the key attractions, and the landscape is laced with quiet roads and footpaths to explore. The variety of the terrain means that routes are available to suit a range of abilities. Horse riding is also an option in many areas, as is hang-gliding. In winter, Tuscany's highest peak Monte Amiata, offers downhill and cross-country skiing.

The main spectator sport is of course football (*calcio*) which is followed avidly. Matches are played in Siena's 10,000-seater stadium, beside the ancient fortress. Siena now plays in the *Serie A*, Italy's premier division.

Cycling

The local tourist board produces a useful brochure on cycling around Siena called *Terre di Siena in Bici* which gives suggested routes to follow: www.terresienainbici.it.

Eco Rent, Via Tosco Romagnola 1321, Casciano, **T** 050 777461, info@ecorent.net. Mountain bikes and scooters for hire. Will deliver.

Val d'Orcia in Mountain Bike, Montalcino, **T** 347 0535638, www.bikemontalcino.it. Guided excursions on mountain bikes in the Val d'Orcia. Length varies from 2½ hours to several days.

Walking and Cycling Agency, Via Ricasoli 26, Siena, **T** 338 8950 100, www.walkingagency.com. You can hire a bike from here or join one of their relaxed, one-day cycling tours.

Football

AC Siena, Via dei Montanini 87, **T** 0577 281084, www.acsiena.it. The local football team play in black and white striped shirts, echoing the stripes that adorn the interior of the Duomo. Their home ground is the Stadio Artemio Franchi, Via dello Stadio. Once struggling to stay in *Serie B*, the club has prospered under new president Paolo De Luca, a Neapolitan businessman and is now in *Serie A* – meaning that fans can watch hotly contested matches against their great rivals from Florence who play in the same division.

Tickets cost upwards of €20 and can be bought from various outlets including:

Tra. In, Piazza Gramsci, **T** 0577 204111; **Fabbri Emanuele**, Via di Pantaneto 154, **T** 0577 284352 and various *tabbachi* such as **Tabaccheria Naghite**, Via Aretina 6, **T** 0577 247641.

Golf

There are two golf clubs and a driving range within easy reach of Siena. A round of golf will cost from about €60 per person.

Golf Club Villa Gori, Via Marciano 18, Siena, **T** 0577 44803. Golf club within hotel complex. *Open all year, Tue-Sun*.

Sant'Andrea Driving Range, Sant'Andrea, San Gimignano, **T** 0577 941173. *Open all year, Tue-Sun*.

Siena Golf Club, Le Segalaie, Via Grosetana 17, Sovicille, near Siena, **T** 0577 348192. *Open all year*. 18 holes.

Gyms

The importance of having a *bella figura* can't be over-stressed. So if the pasta's settling around your waist there are plenty of gyms around the city where you can get a workout.
Future Gym, Via Monte Cengio 21, **T** 0577 41238.
Gold Gym, Via di Fieravecchia 9, **T** 0577 285272.
Gymnica 2000, Via Alessandro VII 36, **T** 0577 588308.
Gymnos, Piazza Provenzano 9, **T** 0577 223159.
Happy Gym, Strada Sant'Eugenia 53, **T** 0577 223848.
Palestra Accademia, Via Mario Mencatelli 5/7, **T** 0577 281081.
Palestra Virtus, Via Vivaldi 28, **T** 0577 221055.
Perfect Body, Strada Massetana 56, **T** 0577 226182.
Physical Center, Via Vallerozzi 13, **T** 0577 48539.
Planet Club, Strada Grossetana 65, **T** 0577 394053.

Hang-gliding

Sienapoint, Via della Sapienza 98, **T** 0577 222684, www.sienapoint.com. Available from April to October at weekends. Fly tandem with a pilot/instructor. Flight lasts from 20 to 60 minutes depending on wind conditions.

Horse riding

Associazione Provinciale dei Cavalieri Senesi, Strade delle Volte alte 39, **T** 339 185 7530 for information, or **T** 340 781 5935 to book. The Sienese Riders' Association is an organization of amateur riders who organize one- or two-day hacks in the countryside around Siena. See also p198.

Tennis

Circolo Tennis La Racchetta, Piazza don Perucatti 1, **T** 0577 221110.
Circolo Tennis San Miniato, Via di Vittoria Giuseppe 12.
Tennis Campansi, Via Campansi 18, **T** 0577 270560.

Skiing

South of the Val d'Orcia is Tuscany's highest mountain, Monte Amiata, over 1,738 m high. This extinct volcano is now a popular skiing area, the focus of activity being the Abbey of San Salvatore. Downhill and cross-country skiing are both available and chairlifts run from Prato delle Macinaie and Prato delle Cantore.

Swimming

There are several public swimming pools in Siena.
Piscina Acquacalda, Via Bianchi, **T** 0577 52667. Indoor pool. Also has an outdoor pool open June to September.
Piscina Amendola, Piazza Amendola, **T** 0577 47496.

Sports

Walking

Tuscany's wooded slopes and rolling hills are covered with walking trails, which are generally marked with a red and white flash – though these can often be hard to spot. Purchase maps from bookshops in Siena or contact the **CAI** (Club Alpino Italiano) www.cai.it. You often get more out of walking with a local guide.

Toscana Adventure Team, Casa Carbona, Via di S Luca, Vinci, **T** 00 39 348 7911 215, www.tateam.it. Walking, cycling and mountain bike tours around Siena with knowledgeable guides.

Viaggio Antico, Via Guarnacci 5, **T** 0588 81527, www.viaggioantico.com. Local guides can show you walks and nature in the Val di Cecina, the undiscovered countryside around Volterra. They also have activities for children.

Wildlife watching

Tuscany is the most wooded part of Italy and has a number of **national parks** and protected **nature reserves** (www.parks.it). They offer plenty of opportunities for cycling, walking and wildlife watching – wolves, mouflon, eagles and wild boar are just some of the creatures that live in these wild spaces. In the northern part of the province of Arezzo is the **Casentinesi National Park**, info@parcoforestecasentinesi.it, which lies on the Appenine ridge and stretches into Emilia-Romagna. In the Province of Siena are several nature reserves, www.riservanaturali.provincia.siena.it, and the Monte Amiata area also has plenty of unspoiled countryside including the **Monte Labbro Reserve** (www.parcofaunistico.it, *closed Mon*). Ask at the tourist office (p27) for further information.

Italy's reputation for being child friendly is well deserved and the Sienese love children as much as any Italian. Siena is also a very safe place. Travellers with children will be welcomed everywhere, and the kids cheerfully clucked over by everyone from elderly ladies to hip young guys. There's no problem taking them into shops or restaurants, and staff smile indulgently, rather than scowl, when you come in; local people frequently eat out with the whole family, their own children usually behaving extremely well. Museums and attractions generally give free entry to under-fives and reductions for older children. Siena's steeply sloping streets can make pushing a buggy an effort and the emphasis on cultural attractions may leave some children yawning. But there are many sights that they'll find fun; visits to traditional craft workshops can go down well and the Campo's an ideal spot for unhurried family picnics. The tourist office has a leaflet, *Trekking for Young Explorers*, describing a city walk especially for children. The countryside offers loads of possibilities for letting off steam, with walks and cycle rides. Many villas also have swimming pools.

Siena

Nurseries

Giocolenuvole, Strada di Monastero 1, **T** 0577 391006.
Southwest Siena **Off map** Playgroup facilities and baby-sitting.

La Casa dei Bimbi, Viale Europa 37, **T** 0577 223024,
www.nascitadolce.it/casabimbi_frame.html *Southeast Siena*
Off map Steiner centre, organic food and baby-sitting service.

Sights

Museo d'Arte per Bambini, Via dei Pispini 164, **T** 0577 46517.
Map 2, C10, p237 Art museum set up especially for children, it
organizes workshops, activities and special exhibitions.

Museo di Storia Naturale, Via Pier Andrea Mattioli. *Sun-Fri
0900-1300, 1500-1800, closed Thu afternoon. Free. Map 2, G4, p236
See also p197* Fossils, rocks, stuffed animals and skeletons,
including an enormous whale.

Orto Botanico, Via Pier Andrea Mattioli 4, **T** 0577 235415.
*Mon-Fri 0800-1230, 1430-1730, Sat 0800-1200. Free. Map 2, H4,
p236 See also p52* The university botanical garden has peaches,
lemons and persimmons hanging from the trees. At the bottom
there's a good spot for a picnic.

Torre del Mangia, Piazza del Campo, **T** 0577 292263.
*Winter 1000-1600 (approx), summer 1000-1900. Map 2, B5, p236
See also p36* Older children might enjoy the novelty of climbing
to the top for great views.

Kids

Shopping

Gulp, Via dei Montanini 85, **T** 0577 288367. *Tue-Sat 0900-1300, 1530-1930, Mon 0900-1300. Map 3, D7, p239* Clothes for newborns to teens in distinctive, frilly Italian style.

Mazzuoli, Via di Città 48, **T** 0577 40123. *Summer Mon-Sat 1000-2000, winter 1000-1300, 1530-1930. Map 2, B4, p236* Posh clothes for kids from seven months to 10 years.

Stampatello, Via di Città 116, **T** 0577 247486. *Mon-Sat 1030-1330, 1500-1900. Map 2, B4, p236* Wooden Pinocchio puppets, toys and pencils.

Around Siena

Activities

For cycling, walking and other activities around Siena, see Sports p189 and Directory p201.

Bagno Vignoni 4 km southeast of San Quirico d'Orcia on the SS2. *See also page 66* The steaming waters of the pool in this hamlet should even interest teenagers. Keep watch over small children, though, as the water is scalding.

Horse riding The following operators specialize in horse riding for children: **Club Ippico Sense**, Loc Pian del Lago, Monteriggioni, **T** 0577 318316, a riding centre; **La Casella Cavalgiocare**, Loc Casella, Sovicille, **T** 0577 314323, www.cavalgiocare.it, based in Montagnola Senese Park, riding and jumping courses; **Scuderia Le Vigne**, Via della

Trove 10, Castelmuzio, Trequanda, **T** 0577 665032, www.scuderielevigne.com, courses for children of 11 and upwards, beginners and more experienced. See also p193.

Nature Train, Val d'Orcia Railway, **T** 0577 207413, www.ferrovieturistiche.it. *Dates of trips vary, check locally.* A train trip usually goes down well. Volunteers run vintage diesel and steam trains that clatter out of Siena and into the countryside.

Sights

Caporciano Mine and Museo delle Miniere Mine 1 km from Montecatini Val di Cecina, **T** 347 8718870. *Easter-Nov, core times Thu, Sat and Sun 1600-1800, tours start at the mine on the hour. €5, €3 for outside area only, €8 including museum in centre of the village. See also p86* Don hard hats and reflective jackets for a guided tour of this copper mine.

Museo del Cristallo, Via dei Fossi 8, Colle di Val d'Elsa, **T** 0577 934035. *Summer daily 1000-1200, 1600-1930, winter closed on Mon. Entry €3. See also p76* Includes a 'crystal forest' with crystals suspended from the ceiling.

Museo del Tartufo, San Giovanni d'Asso **T** 0577 803101. *Weekends 1000-1300, 1400-1800 (approx, hours vary). Beside the castello. See also p67* Some scratch-and-sniff displays that kids will enjoy, as well as a film on truffle hunting.

Museo Etnografico del Bosco, Orgia, Sovicille, **T** 0577 582323. *Fri and Sat 0930-1230. About 12 km south of Siena.* Outdoor woodland museum with forest trails and ancient rural crafts like charcoal burning.

Parco Museo Minerario, Abbadia San Salvatore, **T** 0577 778324, www.museominerario.it. *0900-1300, 1500-2030. Inside the mine, €2.58, outside €1.54. About 1 hr 15 mins' drive south of Siena.* Mining complex at Monte Amiata that's gradually being opened to the public. Tours often available with former miners.

Directory

Airline offices
Air France, **T** 055 284304/5 (Florence); **Alitalia**, **T** 848 865641, or from the UK **T** 0870 608 6001, www.alitalia.it; **T** 39 06 65953880 (Rome Fiumicino). **British Airways T** 1478 12266 (Florence); **Continental**, **T** 06-476-75206 (Rome); **Easy Jet**, **T** 848 887766; Lufthansa, **T** 055-217936 (Florence); **Meridiana**, **T** 39 055 318530 (Florence); **Ryanair**, **T** 899 678910; **Zoom Airlines**, flyzoom.com.

Airport information
Florence Airport (Amerigo Vespucci) **T** 055 315 874, www.aeroporto.firenze.it. **Pisa International Airport** (Galileo Galilei) **T** 050 849 402, www.pisa-airport.com. **Rome Fiumicino Airport** (Leonardo da Vinci; Rome's main airport) **T** 06 65951, www.adr.it. **Rome Ciampino Airport** (GB Pastine; mostly budget carriers) **T** 06 794 941, www.adr.it.

Banks and ATMs
Banks open Mon-Fri 0830-1330, 1430-1530. Cash machines are available at most banks and accept Visa and other international cards.

Bicycle hire
Centro Bici, Via Toselli 110, **T** 0577 282550; **DF Bike**, Via Messetanta Romana 54, **T** 0577 271905; **DF Motor**, Via dei Gazzani 16/18, **T** 0577 288387; **Walking and Cycling Agency**, Via Ricasoli 26, Siena, **T** 338 8950 100, www.walkingagency.com; **Welcome**, Via Simone Martini 18, **T** 0577 282810, www.welcomesiena.com.

Car hire
The following companies have offices in Siena: **Avis**, Via Simone Martini 36, **T** 0577 270305, www.avisautonoleggio.it; **Hertz**, Viale Sardegna 37, **T** 0577 45085, www.hertz.co.uk; **Maggiore**,

Via Mentana 108, **T** 0577 236610, www.maggiore.it; and **Sixt Rent a Car**, Viale Europa 9, **T** 0577 530123.

At Pisa airport you will find several car hire offices in the arrivals hall including **Avis**, **Europcar**, **Liberty Rent International**, **Maggiore** and **Sixt Rent a Car**. Rome's Fiumicino airport also has car hire offices for these companies.

Consulates

Most consulates and embassies are in Rome or Florence.
Australia Embassy in Rome, **T** 06 852721, www.australian-embassy.it. **UK** Consulate, Florence, **T** 055 284133, main embassy in Rome, **T** 06 4220 001; **US** Consulate, Florence, **T** 055 239 8276, main embassy in Rome, **T** 06 46741, www.usis.it. More information at www.embassyworld.com.

Contrade headquarters
Terzo di San Martino

Civetta, Piazzetta del Castellare, **T** 0577 285505, www.civetta.sienanet.it; **Leocorno**, Via di Follonica 15, **T** 0577 49298; **Nicchio**, Via dei Pispini 68, **T** 0577 49600, www.nobilecontradadelnicchio.it; **Valdimontone**, Via di Valdimontone 6, **T** 0577 222590, www.valdimontone.it; **Torre**, Via Salicotto 76, **T** 0577 222181, www.capitanodellatorre.it.

Terzo di Città

Aquila, Casato di Sotto, **T** 0577 288086, www.contradedellaquila.it; **Chiocciola**, Via San Marco 37, **T** 0577 45455, www. chiocciola.org; Onda, Via Giovanni Duprè 111, **T** 0577 48384, www.contradacapitana dellonda; **Pantera**, Via San Quirico, **T** 0577 48468; **Selva**, Piazzetta della Selva, **T** 0577 45093, www.contradadellaselva.it; **Tartuca**, Via Tommaso Pendola 21, **T** 0577 49448, www.tartuca.it.

Terzo di Camollia

Bruco, Via del Comune 44, **T** 0577 44842; **Drago**, Piazza Matteotti 19, **T** 0577 40575, www.contradadeldrago.it; **Giraffa**, Via delle Vergini 18, **T** 0577 287091, www.comune.siena.it/giraffa; **Istrice**, Via Camollia 87, **T** 0577 48495, www.istrice.org; **Lupa**, Via Vallerozzi 71, **T** 0577 286038; **Oca**, Vicolo del Tiratoio 11, **T** 0577 285413, www.contradadelloca.it.

Cookery and craft courses

G&F, Le Bonatte, Loc Le Bonatte, Radda in Chianti, **T** 0577 738783, gioia@chiantinet.it. Can arrange cookery classes in a variety of locations.

Tuscan Tour, **T** 347 143 5004, www.tuscantour.com. Can arrange classes in everything from Italian to working in alabaster.

Vetrate Artistiche, Via della Galluzza, Siena **T** 0577 48033. www.glassisland.com. Mon-Fri 0900-1300, 1500-1800. Stained-glass workshop offering courses ranging from one day to two weeks.

Villa Palagione, Volterra, p116, and **Sant'Anna in Camprena**, Via Don Flori, Pienza, www.scuolacamprena.toscana.nu, see p111, also run courses.

Disabled

Italy is somewhat behind other European countries in catering for disabled people, but Siena makes an effort. Information 'Siena Enabled' is available on the city's website: www.comune.siena.it. Some local guides are able to offer tours in sign language, www.guidesiena.it. Information also from **T** 0577 292215. Some specialist agencies can give more information including: **Accessible Italy**, www.accessibleitaly.com; **Unione Italiana dei Ciechi** (Italian Blind Society), **T** 06 699881, www.uiciechi.it; **SATH** (Society for Accessible Travel and Hospitablity), www.sath.org.

Doctors
Pronto Soccorso, First Aid Department Ospedale Le Scotte, Viale Bracci, Siena **T** 118.

Electricity
Italy uses a 220V mains supply. Bring a continental adaptor that works in both Northern and Southern Europe so you can be sure that one will work.

Emergency numbers
Police T 112 (*carabinieri*), **T** 113 (state police); **Ambulance T** 118, **Fire T** 115; **Emergency breakdown T** 116.

Hospital
The city's main hospital **Le Scotte**, is outside town, past the railway station, at Viale Mario Bracci. **T** 0577 585111. There is an emergency room, **T** 0577 585807, and also a dialysis centre, **T** 0577 586214.

Internet/email
Italian law demands that you must produce ID when using internet cafés, so you may well be asked for your passport – though some places are pretty lax about enforcing this.

    Megaweb, Via di Pantaneto 132, **T** 0577 44946. €3 for 30 mins, but will only charge you for the time you use. **Siena@web** have three outlets in the city: Via di Pantaneto 54, **T** 0577 247460, *Mon-Fri 1000-1900* (also ship goods worldwide and have access for laptops); Via di Città 121, **T** 0577 226366, Mon-Fri 1000-2000, Sat and Sun 1200-2000; Via di Pantaneto 59, Oct-Apr Mon-Fri 0800-2000, Sun 0900-2000 and summer Mon-Fri 0800-2000. €1.50 for 15 mins, €3 for 30 mins and €5 for 11 hr. **Skyweb**, Via del Refe Nero 18, **T** 0577 224266. Internet, fax and digital camera transfer.

Language schools

Università per Stranieri di Siena, Via di Pantaneto 45,
T 0577 240111. **Dante Alighieri**, Via Tommaso Pendola 37,
T 0577 49533, www.dantealighieri.com.

Laundry

Ondablu, Via del Casato di Sotto 17. 0800-2200.
Wash and Dry Lavarapido, Via di Pantaneto. 0800-2200.

Libraries

Biblioteca Comunale degli Intronati, Via della Sapienza 1/7,
T 0577 280704, www.biblioteca.comune.siena.it.

Lost property

Polizia Municipale, Via Tozzi, **T** 0577292588.

Media

English-language and other language newspapers are available
from **Libreria Senese**, Via di Città 64, and from other bookshops
along Via di Città.

Italy's state-run terrestrial television station is **RAI** which has
three channels (1, 2 and 3), while Silvio Berlusconi's **Mediaset** has
Italia Uno, **Rete Quattro** and **Canale Cinque**. Most coverage
seems to be made up of chat shows and game shows, invariably
filled with women wearing miniscule skirts or hot pants.

Main Italian newspapers are **La Repubblica** and **Corriere
della Sera**. **La Nazione** is a Florence-based paper and
Il Vernacoliere is a Tuscan publication.

Pharmacies

Pharmacies include **Antica Farmacia Parenti**, Via Banchi di
Sopra 43, **T** 0577 283269, where people speak English. Among
others are **Ceccherini on the Campo**, and San Girgio at Via
di Pantaneto 75. Pharmacies open late in rotation.

Police

The **police station** can be reached at **T** 0577 201111;
traffic police at **T** 0577 292550.

Post office

The main post office is at Piazza Matteotti 37. Mon-Sat 0815-1900.
Ordinary postage costs from €0.41; priority mail from €0.60.
Information at www.poste.it.

Public holidays

1 Jan – New Year's Day; 6 Jan – Epiphany; Easter Monday;
25 Apr – Liberation Day; 1 May– Labour Day; 2 May – Republic
Day; 2 Jul – Palio (Siena only); 15 Aug – Assumption of the Virgin;
16 Aug – Palio (Siena only); 1 Nov – All Saints' Day; 8 Dec – Feast
of the Immaculate Conception; 25 Dec – Christmas Day; 26 Dec –
St Stephen's Day. Towns and villages also have their own public
holidays on local saints' days.

Religious services

Churches post individual times of services outside.

Taxi firms

There's a taxi rank on Piazza Matteotti and one by the station.
To call a taxi **T** 0577 49222, or 44504.

Telephone

Siena's dialing code is 0577 and you must dial it even within the
city. The prefix for Italy is +39. You do not need to drop the initial
'0' when dailing from abroad. **Directory enquiries T** 12.
International operator assisted service **T** 170.

Time

Italy uses Central European Time, GMT+1. In the summer it's
GMT+2.

Tipping

Tipping isn't obligatory, but is appreciated – check whether a service charge has been included in the bill. It's common to round up taxi fares and when paying for a cup of coffee.

Toilets

The most convenient public toilets are on Via di Beccheria, close to the Campo. There's a charge of 50 cents. Other toilets are in La Lizza subway (under the bus station in Piazza Gramsci), 50 cents, and also at Via del Casato di Sotto, 80 cents.

Transport enquiries

Piazza Gramsci, information is available at the centre in the underpass, below the piazza.

Blue **SITA** buses (www.sita-on-line.it); Terravision, www.Terravision.it; **SENA** bus (**T** 800 930960, or 0577 283203, www.sena.it); **Vola in Bus** (Fly by Bus) service, www.ataf.net.

Train information, www.trenitalia.it.

Travel agents

Asso Di Cuori Travel & Tourism SRL, Via Cecco Angiolieri 24 **T** 0577 287890. There are also agents along Via dei Montanini and Via di Camollia.

Background

209

A sprint through history

c700 BC According to legend, Siena is founded by the sons of Remus, Aschius and Senius, who fled to Tuscany to escape their uncle Romulus. Historical evidence suggests it was an Etruscan settlement – home to an Etruscan family 'Seina'.

27-14 BC The Roman Emperor Augustus establishes a military camp, *Sena Julia*, on high ground in Siena.

774 Tuscany becomes a distinct region during the reign of Charlemagne.

AD 990 Sigeric, Archbishop of Canterbury travels to Rome along the Via Francigena, establishing it as a path for pilgrims. Siena is an important halt.

c1125 Siena becomes a free republic.

1137 Siena acquires valuable silver mines at Montieri.

1150-1220 Siena expands to encompass the hamlet of Camollia, creating the Terzo di Camollia, and extends southeast around Castel Montone, forming the Terzo di San Martino. The city now resembles a three-pointed star.

1240 Siena University is inaugurated.

1260 Tuscany is torn by battles between Guelph and Ghibelline factions. Siena is now an important banking centre and home to rich noble families. The city, which is Ghibelline, defeats Guelph Florence at the Battle of Montaperti.

1269 Florentine Guelphs defeat Siena at the Battle of Colle di Val d'Elsa.

1287	Siena, by now Guelph, institutes the Council of Nine, a new form of government made up of the merchant classes and excluding nobles. Under this stable regime the city prospers, major building projects take place and the arts flourish.
1347	Catherine of Siena is born in the Contrada dell'Oca (Goose). She has visions as a child and takes a vow of virginity.
1348	The Black Death sweeps through Siena, killing almost two-thirds of the population.
1355	A revolt of the nobles ends the government of 'the Nine'.
1371	Wool workers rebel in the Bruco Rising. They take the Palazzo Pubblico but are soon suppressed. Years of instability and infighting follow.
1380	Catherine of Siena dies in Rome.
1399-1404	Siena briefly submits to the rule of Gian Galeazzo Visconti, Duke of Milan, with whom it is allied against Florence. The city reclaims its freedom after his death and power struggles resume.
1458	Enea Silvius, a member of the wealthy Sienese Piccolomini family, becomes Pope Pius II. He creates his ideal Renaissance city, Pienza, and commissions major buildings in Siena.
1461	Catherine of Siena is canonized.
1487-1524	Ruthless nobleman Pandolfo Petrucci 'Il Magnifico' takes control of Siena. He rules until his death and is followed by his son.

Background

1530	The Emperor Charles V establishes a garrison of Spanish troops in Siena who impose their stamp on life in the city. The Spanish introduce the Inquisition and educated people and artists flee.
1552	Infuriated that they've been made to pay for the new Spanish fortress in the city, Siena allies itself with France, Charles V's enemy. The Spanish are driven from the city.
1554	Siena is besieged by Charles' Imperial troops and Florentine forces, who lay waste the surrounding countryside and torture local people.
1554	Having endured months of starvation, Siena surrenders. However, a large group of citizens leave and set up a 'Republic of Siena' in Montalcino.
1557	Charles' son Phillip II sells Siena to Cosimo de' Medici, Duke of Florence.
1559	With the end of the resistance at Montalcino, Siena's independence ends for good; it becomes subsumed into the Florentine Medici State and part of the Duchy of Tuscany. The city declines.
1656	The Palio is run for the first time in its current form. It incorporates two races, one run 'on the straight', usually reserved for nobles, and the other run 'in the round' on the Campo, in which the *contrade* competed.
1808	Tuscany becomes part of the Napoleonic empire.
1815	Napoleon is defeated at the Battle of Waterloo.
1830s	Siena, with its once unfashionable medieval architecture, becomes an important stopping point on the Grand Tour.

1848	First War of Italian Independence.
1859	Second War of Independence under Garibaldi. Siena is the first city in Tuscany to vote for annexation to Italy.
1861	Proclamation of the unified Kingdom of Italy.
1922	Start of the Facist regime under Mussolini.
1941	Italy enters the Second World War as a German ally.
1943	Mussolini is deposed and Italy signs an armistice. Nazis occupy Italy and partisans fight in countryside around Siena.
July 1944	Troops of the French Expeditionary forces liberate Siena.
1946	Italy becomes a Republic. Post-war Siena has a left-wing administration.
1950s	Crisis in the countryside as agricultural share-croppers leave the land.
1970 and 1980s	British middle-classes buy abandoned properties in Chianti. Tourism grows.
2001	Controversial tycoon Silvio Berlusconi becomes Prime Minister of Italy.
2005	Siena's Palazzo Chigi Saracini opens to visitors (from January to June) for the first time for 200 years. Cigarette smoking is banned in all public places in tobacco-loving Italy. Plain clothes officers enforce the ban and hefty fines apply.

Art and architecture

c700 BC   According to legend, Siena's founders, the sons of Remus, bring with them the statue of Rome's she-wolf suckling the twins. It becomes the symbol of Siena. Senius is said to build a castle, Castelsenio, later known as Castelvecchio, the nucleus of the city. Their uncle Romulus sends the soldier Camulius to capture them. He pitches camp in an area that became known as Camollia. History, rather than myth, gives the city Etruscan origins.

27-14 BC   The Romans build a military camp in Siena. The forum is the site of today's Campo.

10th century   Pilgrims following the Via Francigena to Rome pass Siena, walking along the Via Camollia. Churches, taverns and hostels began to spring up to serve them. The church of San Pietro dates back to this time.

1090   First recorded references to the Spedale di Santa Maria della Scala, the pilgrims' hospital. During the 11th century Siena expands to encompass Camollia and other hamlets. The number of pilgrims visiting the city continues to grow and by 1288 there are around 90 hostels in the city.

1179   The Duomo – Cathedral – is consecrated, built near Castelvecchio on the site of an earlier church.

13th century   The Duomo is enlarged and embellished. Nicola and Giovanni Pisano create an elaborate façade; Nicola and his assistants carve the magnificent marble pulpit (1265-1268). Under the Council of Nine (see p211), art and architecture flourish. In the latter part of the century the Palazzo Pubblico is constructed, and

	Italian Gothic buildings fill the city. The Sienese School of Painting evolves from Byzantine roots.
1308-1311	Duccio di Buoninsegna paints the *Maestà* for the high altar of the Duomo. It is now in the Museo dell'Opera del Duomo.
1312-1315	Simone Martini paints his *Maestà* on the wall of the Sala del Mappamondo in the Palazzo Pubblico. It breathes new life and realism into Sienese painting.
1337-1339	Ambrogio Lorenzetti is commissioned by the Council of Nine to fresco the walls of the Palazzo Pubblico with the *Allegories of Good and Bad Government*. The paintings deal with secular, political themes and also depict landscapes.
1340s	The Campo is completed, part of the Council of Nine's plan to create an ordered, coherent city. Plans are made to create an even greater cathedral and work begins on an extension. But the Black Death of 1348 causes an economic crisis, and reduces the population to such an extent that the work is abandoned. It heralds the ending of the distinctive Sienese School of art.
1369	Work starts on creating a marble *pavimento* on the floor of the Duomo. Some of the city's greatest artists were involved in its creation.
1409-1419	Jacopo della Quercia carves the grand marble fountain, the Fonte Gaia, for the Campo.
1440-44	The walls of Santa Maria della Scala hospital are covered with frescoes by Il Vecchietta and other artists. The frescoes do not depict religious subjects but the daily life of the hospital.

c1445	Renaissance painter Piero della Francesca, from Sansepolcro, covers the walls of San Francesco church in Arezzo with frescoes depicting *The Legend of the True Cross*.
c1450-68	Piero della Francesca paints the *Madonna del Parto* in Monterchi; it shows Mary heavily pregnant.
1497	Luca Signorelli starts to paint the cloisters of Monte Oliveto Maggiore with frescoes of the *Life of St Benedict*. When he fails to complete the work Il Sodoma (p73) continues the task.
1505-1507	*Pinturicchio* paints the walls of the Piccolomini Library in the Duomo with a fresco cycle illustrating the life of Pope Pius II.
1547	The carved marble floor of the Duomo is finally completed.
1560	The Fortezza (fortress) is built by Cosimo de' Medici after Siena comes under Florentine rule and becomes part of the Duchy of Tuscany.
17th-18th centuries	Siena declines, the population shrinks and it becomes neglected. Lack of development preserves its unfashionable, medieval Gothic buildings.
20th century	Siena's buildings emerge largely unscathed from the Second World War. In the 1980s work begins on restoring Santa Maria della Scala's unique frescoes. In 1999 a 'crypt' is discovered squeezed between the Duomo and the Baptistry. The walls are covered with 13th-century frescoes.
2004	Restoration work reveals medieval frescoes on the walls of Santa Maria della Scala. They had been plastered over when it was a hospital.

A poor man's feast

The Italian nickname for Tuscans is *mangiafagioli* – 'bean eaters', a disparaging reference to the region's traditional reliance on beans as a staple foodstuff. And there's no doubt this humble ingredient plays a major role in Tuscan cuisine, which is essentially rustic in character. But don't think this means you won't eat well here. Tuscans take their food as seriously as they take their appearance – more so in fact – and the style of cooking cleverly combines extreme simplicity with great sophistication. Throughout Tuscany you will find dishes based primarily on a few simple, and extremely fresh, ingredients prepared in such a way as to highlight their respective flavours. Slow cooking is a feature; nothing is rushed and dishes are eaten separately so that you can fully appreciate what you're eating. When you order a plate of beans you get just that, beans; your salad or meat would comprise another course.

Traditional Tuscan cuisine is a *cucina povera*, or 'poor man's cuisine' since, until recent years at least, most people survived on whatever they could grow, hunt or gather. Not too difficult given the productiveness of the landscape, with its fertile fields, dense woodlands filled with chestnuts and mushrooms, abundant herbs, and numerous animals like wild boars and rabbits. Nothing ever went to waste, and even today everything from calves' tongues and brains, to tripe and pigs' trotters are still painstakingly turned into meals. Yet although meat features prominently, Tuscan food is excellent for vegetarians and many dishes are entirely vegetable or bean based.

Some of the richer dishes you'll find on menus have their roots in the courts of the Medici and other noble families. There's *cinghiale in dolce e forte*, for instance, which is wild boar in a 'strong and sweet' sauce with chocolate, vinegar, pine nuts, raisins and rosemary – invented by Florentine chefs during the Renaissance it's the sort of thing you can imagine Henry VIII tucking into.

Even some dishes that are usually considered French have Tuscan origins: crêpes, onion soup and béchamel sauce were taken to France by the chefs of Caterina de' Medici when her court moved to France in the 16th century.

A Tuscan meal usually starts with *crostini* (toasted bread topped with something like *fegatini* – liver pâté) and *affettati* (an assortment of cold cuts such as *proscuitto* and salami). Look out for toppings of *lardo di Colonnata* too, it's seasoned pork fat from northern Tuscany. However, the favourite starter, *fettunta*, is simplicity itself: literally 'greasy slice', it consists of toasted bread rubbed with a clove of garlic and topped with olive oil, preferably the freshest available. Local *pecorino* cheese features on many menus too.

Soups are a big deal: hearty, filling and virtually a meal in themselves; *zuppa di faro e fagioli* (bean and barley), for instance, or a simple bean soup. Many are made with bread. Tuscan bread is unsalted and, as it goes hard rather than stale or mouldy when it's a few days old, poor families could use it up in a variety of ways. You'll often see *pappa al pomodoro* (bread in tomato sauce) or *ribollita* (literally 'reboiled'), a bread, bean and vegetable soup. (If you dunk hunks of bread when you're eating it, the locals will think you're mad.)

Pasta – typically *penne*, long flat *pappardelle*, or filled ravioli – is generally served with fresh *porcini* mushrooms, a simple tomato sauce or a sauce made with wild boar, rabbit or hare. In Siena you'll often see *pici*, a sort of thick spaghetti made with wheat or semolina flour and water. It's usually eaten with *ragù*, a slow cooked meaty sauce.

Tuscany's most famous meat dish is *bistecca alla fiorentina*, which is grilled rare or medium and is usually served for a minimum of two people (who might be advised to get a new mortgage to pay for it). Favourite meats in Siena come from Chianina cattle, raised on the flat lands around Cortona, and from

The wine of friendship

While you're in Siena make sure you try some *vin santo*, a dark, sweet fortified wine that tastes a bit like sherry. The name means 'holy wine' as it used to be used by the priest for Holy Communion – the local joke was that while he was holding it up and making the sign of the cross he was secretly inspecting the quality and hoping the congregation would leave some for him. Today it's generally considered the wine of friendship. Many people still make it at home and it's often offered to guests. Grapes are dried in a windy room for three months, then pressed and the juice put in a barrel or *carratello* to ferment. This contains the *mama* – the sediment from the last production. It's then placed in a loft and left to age with the seasons. It gets no special treatment and is exposed to extremes of temperature – by the time it's ready, a bottle can stay open for months without spoiling.

Cinta Senese pigs (black pigs with a distinctive white band). A typical fish is *baccalà* (salt-cod), often served with tomato sauce.

Vegetables are a strong point. You'll be able to try everything from spinach to *cavolo nero* (black cabbage). And then there are beans, of course: *cannellini*, *borlotti*, the rare *zolfino* (a tiny white bean) and Hannibal Lector's favourite, *baccelli* (fava) beans. They're often served on their own, stewed for hours with tomatoes and fragrant sage leaves.

Dessert is usually something simple like fruit, or *cantuccini* (often sold as *biscotti* overseas), hard dry biscuits that are dunked into *vin santo*, a sweet wine (see box, above). Sienese cakes are distinctive and delicious – make sure you buy them freshly made. *Cavallucci* (the name means 'little horses' as they were originally destined for those who worked in the stables) are dense, aniseed-flavoured buns with candied fruits, while *ricciarelli* are deliciously chewy almond biscuits. The traditional Christmas cake is *panforte*, a stick-to-your-ribs mix of honey, dried fruits and almonds – you'll also find a version made with cinnamon and nutmeg called *panpepato*. Look for *Pan coi Santi* too: it's a spicy loaf with dried fruit and nuts that's only made around All Saints' Day.

Wine accompanies most meals, of course. It's been made in Tuscany since Etruscan times and locals take their wines (which are mainly red) very seriously. Variations in terrain, soil and climate in the Sienese countryside means that many different types are produced within a relatively small area. Most are made with varieties of Sangiovese grapes and are now highly rated by wine experts; the days when Chianti was valued mainly for its handy – wouldn't-it-make-a-good-lampshade – raffia-wrapped bottle are long gone.

The government controls and classifies wines through a system that regulates everything from the types of grapes used to the method of production. Categories start with no-nonsense *vino da tavola* (table wine), followed by IGT (*Indicazione Geografica Tipica*). Next up the scale are DOC (*Denominazione di Origine Controllata*) wines and finally DOCG (*Denominazione di Origine Controllata e Garantita*) – you can easily recognize these as they'll have a small pink tag on the top.

DOCG wines are determined by the grape varieties used, production methods and geographical area. Look out for the famed, and famously pricey, *Brunello di Montalcino*, *Carmignano*, *Chianti*, *Chianti Classico*, *Nobile di Montepulciano* and, the only white in the list, *Vernaccia di San Gimignano*, which was served at Royal weddings in Renaissance times. New kids on the block are the SuperTuscan wines: made from non-indigenous grape varieties like Merlot and Cabernet, they've been produced to create a new type of Italian wine with wide appeal. They're now going at higher prices than traditional DOCG wines. But don't worry too much about labels, just taste a few and make up your own mind.

Books

Travel writing

Although Siena doesn't feature quite as much as Florence or Rome in Victorian accounts of the Grand Tour, it still made a distinct impression on early visitors and receives some evocative mentions. In the late 20th century, a rash of books came out by people who had fulfilled the middle-class dream, left their noisy cities and gone to live in Tuscany.

Dickens, C, *Pictures from Italy* (Penguin 1866). An elegant and observant account of a 19th-century Grand Tour through Italy.

James, H, *Italian Hours* (Penguin 1995, first published 1909). A collection of essays covering the novelist's travels in Italy at the turn of the 20th century. He turns a keen and enthusiastic eye on art, life and culture.

Lawrence, DH, *Etruscan Places* (Penguin, first published 1927). Wandering through tombs in Italy's ancient Etruscan cities, Lawrence gives a voice to a vanished people.

Morton, H V, *A Traveller in Italy* (1930s). The last of the gentlemen travellers, this account of travels in 1950s Italy has enduring appeal and vivid descriptions of places and people.

Fiction and autobiographical accounts

Dusi, I, *Vanilla Beans and Brodo* (Pocket Books 2001). Enjoyable account of how a couple from Australia sell up and make a new life in Montalcino.

Forster, EM, *Where Angels Fear to Tread* (Penguin 2004, first published 1905). Tragi-comic novel following the consequences of a middle-class English woman's love affair with an Italian.

Mayes, F, *Under the Tuscan Sun* (Bantam 1998) and *Bella Tuscany* (Bantam 2000). Bestselling memoirs of how an American woman renovates a villa near Cortona. Evoking the gently rural life, they're a Tuscan version of Peter Mayle's *A Year in Provence*.

Mortimer, J, *Summer's Lease* (Penguin 1988). Middle-class Brits rent a holiday village in Tuscany. The book that embedded Chiantishire in the imagination.

Origo, I, *War in Val d'Orcia* (1947). A war diary of life in the Val d'Orcia from 1943-1944.

Ondaatje, M, *The English Patient* (Picador). A badly burned man is nursed in an Italian monastery in the Second World War.

Vigano, R, *Partisan Wedding* (University of Missouris Press 1999). Vivid writing based on the real experiences of the author and other female members of the Italian Resistance in the Second World War.

Non-fiction

Barzini, L, *The Italians* (Penguin, first published 1964). An Italian gives an incisive portrait of the morals and manners of his countrymen.

Dundes, A and **Falassi**, A, *La Terra in Piazza* (University of California Press, 1975). Extremely informative account of the Palio and what it means to the Sienese.

Jones, T, *The Dark Heart of Italy* (Faber and Faber 2003). Fascinating appraisal of Berlusconi's Italy and the murkier aspects of life.

Language

Italy is a relatively newly united country and this is evident in the strong regional dialects that still exist. In medieval times the most influential writers, Petrarch, Boccaccio and above all Dante, wrote in the Tuscan dialect, thus establishing it as the language of literature, and later the country's official language, the equivalent of English received pronunciation. It is often said that if you wish to learn Italian you should go to Tuscany.

In hotels and bigger restaurants, you'll usually find English is spoken. However, if you are planning to travel off the beaten track, a working knowledge of Italian is extremely useful.

Pronunciation

Stress generally falls on the second-last syllable, as in 'spa-*ghet*-ti'. When a word has an accent, the stress falls on that syllable, as in cit-tà, 'city'.

a short like 'a' in 'cat' or long like 'a' in 'father'
e (è) short like 'e' in 'set', (é) long like 'a' in 'say
i like 'e' in 'meet'
o short like 'o' in 'dot' or long like 'o' in 'hope'
u as in 'oo' in 'book' or 'w' in 'well'
c before *e* or *i*, like 'ch' in chin, otherwise, like 'c' in cat

ch like the 'c' in 'cat'
g before *e* or *i*, like the 'g' in gymnastics, otherwise like 'g' in go
gli as the 'lli' in 'million'
gn as the 'ny' in 'canyon'
h always silent
r a rolled 'rr' sound
sc before *e* or *i*, like 'sh' in sheep, otherwise like 'sk' in skip
z like 'ts' in 'lights' except at the beginning of a word, when it's 'ds' as in 'suds'

Numbers

1 *uno*, 2 *due*, 3 *tre*, 4 *quattro*, 5 *cinque*, 6 *sei*, 7 *sette*, 8 *otto*,
9 *nove*, 10 *dieci*, 11 *undici*, 12 *dodici*, 13 *tredici*, 14 *quattordici*,
15 *quindici*, 16 *sedici*, 17 *diciassette*, 18 *diciotto*, 19 *diciannove*,
20 *venti*, 21 *ventuno*, 22 *ventidue*, 30 *trenta*, 40 *quaranta*,
50 *cinquanta*, 60 *sessanta*, 70 *settanta*, 80 *ottanta*, 90 *novanta*,
100 *cento*, 200 *due cento*, 1000 *mille*.

Basics

hello/hi *ciao/salve*
good day (until after lunch/mid-afternoon) *buongiorno*
good evening (after lunch) *buonasera*
goodnight *buonanotte*
goodbye *arrivederci/ciao (informal)/arrivederla (formal)*
please *per favore*
thank you *grazie*
I'm sorry *mi dispiace*
excuse me *permesso*
you're welcome *prego*
it doesn't matter *non importa*
yes/no *sí/no*

Conversation

alright *va bene*
right then *allora*
who knows! *bo!/chi sa?*
good luck! *in bocca al lupo!* (literally, 'in the mouth of the wolf')
one moment *un'attimo*
hello (when answering the phone) *pronto* (literally, 'ready')
let's go! *andiamo!*
enough/stop *basta!*
I like... *mi piace...*
how's it going? (well, thanks) *come va?* (*bene grazie*)
how are you? *come sta/stai?* (polite/informal)

Questions

how? *come?*
how much? *quanto?*
when? *quando?*
where? *dove?*
why? *perché?*
what? *che cosa?*

Problems

I don't understand *non capisco*
I don't speak Italian *non parlo italiano*
how do you say … (in Italian)? *nome si dice… (in italiano)?*
do you speak English? *parla inglese?*

Getting around

where is…? *dov'è…?*
how do I get to…? *como posso andare a…?*
I want to go to *vorrei andare a…*
do you stop at…? *ferma a…?*
one ticket for… *un biglietto per…*
how much is the ticket? *quant'è il biglietto?*
single *solo andata*
return *andata e ritorno*
does this go to Siena? *questo va a Siena*
airport *aeroporto*
bus stop *fermata*
train *treno*
car *macchina*
taxi *tassì*

Accommodation

a double/single room *una camera doppia/singola*
a double bed *un letto matrimoniale*
for one night/week *per una notte/settimana*

bathroom *bagno*
can I see the room? *posso vedere la camera?*
what time is breakfast? *a che ora è la colazione?*

Eating out
can I have the bill? *posso avere il conto?/Il conto per favore*
what's this? *cos'è questo?*
is there a menu? *c'è un menù?*
where's the toilet? *dov'è il bagno?*

Shopping
this one/that one *questo/quello*
less/more *meno/di più*
how much is it/are they? *quanto costa/costano?*
can I have...? *posso avere...?*

Time
morning *mattina*
afternoon *pommeriggio*
evening *sera*
night *notte*
soon *presto/fra poco*
later *più tardi*
what time is it? *che ore sono?*
today/tomorrow/yesterday *oggi/domani/ieri*

Index

Credits

Footprint credits

Editor: Felicity Laughton
Map editor: Sarah Sorensen
Picture editor: Claire Benison
Publisher: Patrick Dawson
Series created by: Rachel Fielding
In-house cartography: Claire Benison,
Kevin Feeney, Angus Dawson, Esther
Monzón, Thom Wickes
Consultant: Rachel Fielding
Design: Mytton Williams
Maps: Footprint Handbooks Ltd

Photography credits

Front cover: Alamy
Inside colour: Alamy, Julius Honnor,
Powerstock. Inside black and white:
p1 Column in Piazza del Duomo (Alamy);
p5 and p29 Detail of Duomo (Alamy);
p61 Montepulciano (Julius Honnor)
Generic images: John Matchett
Back cover: Alamy

Print

Manufactured in Italy by LegoPrint
Pulp from sustainable forests

Footprint feedback

We try as hard as we can to make
each Footprint guide as up to date as
possible but, of course, things always
change. If you want to let us know
about your experiences – good, bad
or ugly – then don't delay, go to
www.footprintbooks.com and send
in your comments.
® Footprint Handbooks and the Footprint
mark are a registered trademark of
Footprint Handbooks Ltd

Publishing information

Footprint Siena & the heart of Tuscany
1st edition
Text and maps
© Footprint Handbooks Ltd
April 2005

ISBN: 1 904777 32 5
CIP DATA: a catalogue record for this
book is available from the British Library

Published by Footprint Handbooks
6 Riverside Court
Lower Bristol Road
Bath, BA2 3DZ, UK
T +44 (0)1225 469141
F +44 (0)1225 469461
discover@footprintbooks.com
www.footprintbooks.com

Distributed in the USA by
Publishers Group West

Complete title list

(P) denotes pocket guide

Latin America & Caribbean

Antigua & Leeward
 Islands (P)
Argentina
Barbados (P)
Bolivia
Brazil
Caribbean Islands
Central America & Mexico
Chile
Colombia
Costa Rica
Cuba
Cusco & the Inca Trail
Dominican Republic (P)
Ecuador & Galápagos
Havana (P)
Mexico
Nicaragua
Peru
Rio de Janeiro (P)
South American Handbook
St Lucia (P)
Venezuela

North America

New York (P)
Vancouver (P)
Western Canada

Middle East

Dubai (P)
Jordan
Syria & Lebanon

Africa

Cape town (P)
East Africa
Egypt
Libya
Marrakech (P)
Morocco
Namibia
South Africa
Tunisia
Uganda

Australasia

Australia
East Coast Australia
New Zealand
Sydney (P)
West Coast Australia

Asia

Bali
Bhutan
Cambodia
Goa
Hong Kong (P)
India
Indian Himalaya
Indonesia
Laos
Malaysia
Nepal
Northern Pakistan
Rajasthan
Singapore
South India
Sri Lanka
Sumatra
Thailand
Tibet
Vietnam

Europe

Andalucía
Barcelona (P)
Berlin (P)
Bilbao (P)
Bologna (P)
Britain
Cardiff (P)
Copenhagen (P)
Croatia
Dublin (P)
Edinburgh (P)
England
Glasgow (P)
Ireland
London (P)
Madrid (P)
Naples (P)
Northern Spain
Paris (P)
Reykjavik (P)
Scotland
Scotland Highlands
 & Islands
Spain
Tallin (P)
Turin (P)
Turkey
Valencia (P)
Verona (P)

Backpacker

Belize, Guatemala &
 Southern Mexico
Patagonia
Peru, Bolivia & Ecuador

Lifestyle

Surfing Europe
Surfing Britain

Map 1 Siena

Map symbols

☐ Bus station
✝ Cathedral, church
🏛 Museum
✉ Post office
✡ Synagogue
🔲 Tourist information
⬇ Related map
▮ Detail map

234

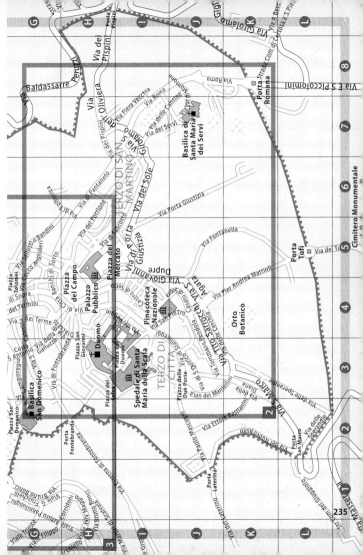

235

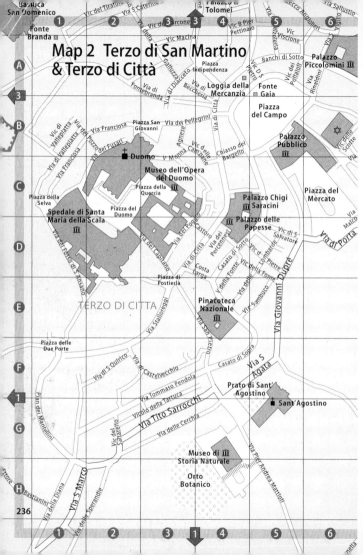

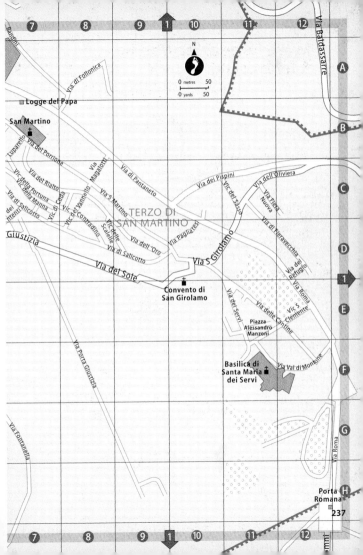

N

0 metres 50

0 yards 50

Via Baldassarre

■ Logge del Papa

San Martino

Via del Porrione

Luparello

Via della Fortuna

Vic della Manna

Via di Salicotto

del Contenti

Vic di Coda

Vic del Vannello

Vic di Contradino

Via S Martino

Via del Rialto

Via di Pantaneto

Via di Follonica

Bandini

Via delle Scuole

Via dell'Oro

Via di Salicotto

Via Pagliaresi

TERZO DI SAN MARTINO

Via dei Pispini

Via dell'Oliviera

Vic del Sasso

Via S Girolamo

Via di Fieravecchia

Fhea Nuova

Via del Refugio

Via Roma

Giustizia

Via del Sole

Convento di San Girolamo

Via dei Servi

Via delle Cantine

Vic S Clemente

Via Porta Giustizia

Piazza Alessandro Manzoni

Basilica di Santa Maria dei Servi

Via Val di Montone

Via Fontanella

Via Roma

Porta Romana

237

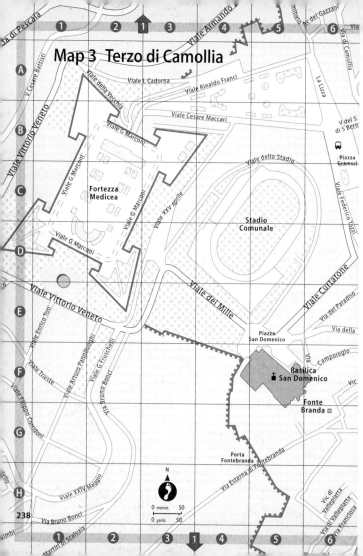

Map 3 Terzo di Camollia

Via di Pescaia

Viale Armando

Vittoria

Av del Gazzani

Via

Via di Camollia

A

V Cesare Battisti

Viale L. Cadorna

Viale Rinaldo Franci

La Lizza

Viale della Vecchia

Viale Cesare Maccari

B

Viale G Marconi

V del S di S Bern

Piazza Gramsci

Viale Vittorio Veneto

Viale dello Stadio

Viale G Marconi

C

Fortezza Medicea

Viale G Marconi

Viale XXV Aprile

Stadio Comunale

Viale Federico Tozzi

D

Viale G Marconi

Viale Vittorio Veneto

Viale der Mille

Viale Curtatone

E

Viale Enrico Toti

Via del Paradiso

Via della

Piazza San Domenico

F

Viale Trieste

Viale Arturo Pampaloni

Viale G Fruschelli

Via Bruno Bonci

Via Camporegio

Basilica San Domenico

Vic

G

Viale Filippo Corridoni

Fonte Branda

H

Viale XXIV Maggio

Porta Fontebranda

Via Esterna di Fontebranda

Vic di Vallepiatta

0 metres 50

0 yards 50

238

Via Bruno Bonci

Via di Vallepiatta

Via Franciosa

Martini di Scalvaia

imbi

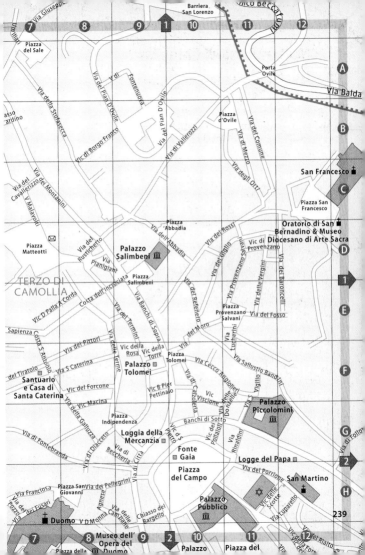

For a different view…
choose a Footprint

Over 100 Footprint travel guides
Covering more than 150 of the world's most exciting
countries and cities in Latin America, the Caribbean, Africa, Indian
sub-continent, Australasia, North America, Southeast Asia, the
Middle East and Europe.

Discover so much more…
The finest writers. In-depth knowledge. Entertaining and accessible.
Critical restaurant and hotels reviews. Lively descriptions of all the
attractions. Get away from the crowds.